Bram Stoker's Dracula: A Study Guide for A Level

Bram Stoker's *Dracula*: A Study Guide for A Level

Contents

	Page
General Introduction	3
Part One: Contexts of Production	5
1.1 Introducing Contexts	9
1.2 Historical Contexts: the *fin-de-siècle*	14
1.3 Social Contexts: The New Woman	19
1.4 Literary Contexts: Imperial Gothic	24
Part Two: Introducing Critical Approaches	33
2.1 Narrative and Structure	35
2.2 Characterisation	42
2.3 Themes and Symbolism	54
2.4 Settings - Crossing Boundaries	62
2.5 The 'Other'	65
Part Three: Textual Commentary and Analysis	68
3.1 "*Our ways are not your ways*": Chapters 1-4	70
3.2 "*Tell me all the news when you write....*": Chapters 5-7	89
3.3 "*So far there is much that is strange*": Chapters 8-16	99
3.4 "*Your girls that you all love are mine already*": Chapters 17-23	113
3.5 "*We shall follow him, and we shall not flinch...*": Chapters 24-27	129
Part Four: Contexts of Reception	139
4.1 Contemporary Reception	142
4.2 Genre-Based and Structuralist Approaches	148
4.3 Psychoanalytical and Gendered Readings	157
4.4 Historicist and Post-Colonial Readings	167
Appendices	177
Examples of Examination Tasks	178
References for Wider Reading	185

General Introduction

Bram Stoker's *Dracula*: A Study Guide for A Level

This study guide will assist you in your GCE A Level study of the novel *Dracula*. The guide can provide support for both the English Literature and the English Language and Literature specifications.

Aims and objectives of Advanced Level GCE English

When engaging with literary texts in Advanced Level study, you will be required to show knowledge and understanding of:

- how writers use language, form and structure to shape meanings and evoke responses in the reader
- how to make connections and explore relationships between a range of literary texts
- the contexts in which texts have been produced and received, and how these contexts influence meaning
- ways of reading and experiencing texts critically and creatively
- how attitudes and values are expressed in texts
- how to communicate fluently, accurately and effectively
- use critical concepts and terminology with discrimination.

Studying GCE English Literature texts

This study guide has been written to provide a rewarding experience for those who are, or are interested in, studying English Literature texts. In particular, this study guide will assist you in understanding and examining Bram Stoker's *Dracula*.

Who is this study guide for?

This study guide is intended to offer a satisfying experience for those learners who undertake an AS or A level qualification in English Literature or English Language and Literature. These qualification pathways are offered by most examination boards, and this resource is primarily designed to assist those who are studying this topic for a GCE qualification, but it may also provide support for those embarking on undergraduate study of *Dracula*.

This study guide will help to lay a sound foundation for those who go on to study English Literature and late Victorian prose at a higher (degree) level, as well as appeal to those who are interested in learning more about the work of Bram Stoker and, in particular, *Dracula*.

Examination Boards

This product is designed to be used as a study aid to support learners in their preparation for the following examination units;

OCR Literature H472/02: Comparative and contextual study
EDEXCEL Literature 8ET02 Prose
EDEXCEL Literature 9ET02 Prose
AQA Language and Literature 7706/1 Views and Voices
AQA Language and Literature 7706/2 Imagining worlds
CCEA Unit AS 2: The Study of Prose Pre 1900

It can also provide useful support for non-examined assessment which requires study of pre-1900 prose fiction, including:

EDUQAS Literature Component 4 Prose Study
WJEC Literature Component 5 Prose Study
WJEC Language and Literature Component 5 Genre Study

Which edition of *Dracula* should I use?

This study guide does not recommend a specific edition of *Dracula*. There are some variations in editions. When preparing for examination, care should be taken that you reference the 1897 publication. This is significantly shorter than the 1911 re-release, which also contains the story *Dracula's Guest*. Popular editions are produced by Wordsworth, Penguin and Norton.

A free online version of the text can be obtained from Project Gutenberg at:

http://www.gutenberg.org/ebooks/345

Bram Stoker's Dracula: A Study Guide for A Level

Using this guide

The text is considered in the wider contexts in which it was written and has been received. The guide is presented in four parts:

Part One

Contexts of Production: considers the writer's life and times, with a focus on significant historical, social and literary contexts.

Part Two

Introduces some critical approaches, including exploration of; narrative, characterisation, structure, key themes and relevant critical ideas.

Part Three

This provides detailed commentary and analysis of each chapter.
This includes relevant background information and reading tasks to enhance understanding.

Part Four

Contexts of Reception: examines how the text was initially received, as well as providing a critical overview of a range of interpretations and approaches.

Please note that direct quotations from the novel and critical works appear in *italics*.

Part One: Contexts of Production

**Part One:
Contexts of Production**

1.1　Introducing Contexts
1.2　Historical Contexts: the fin-de-siècle
1.3　Social Contexts : Fear of the New Woman
1.4　Literary Contexts: Urban and Imperial Gothic

1.1 Introducing Contexts

In this section we will;
- *Demonstrate understanding of the significance and influence of the contexts in which Dracula was written and received*
- *Explore connections across literary texts and contexts*
- *To consider wider social and historical contexts*

Introducing Contexts

When approaching a text at A level, students should consider the contexts of reception and production, and how these may affect the way texts are interpreted. Some of the contexts which may prove relevant to the study of the novel are outlined below. These include:

- *context of writing*
- *context of reading*
- *contexts of time and place*
- *social and cultural contexts*

Social and cultural contexts and contexts of time and place will be discussed throughout the detailed commentary and analysis sections.

As part of your A Level study you are required to consider the wider social, historical and literary contexts of a text, that is, the world in which it is produced and received.

At the close of the twentieth century, there were some critics who either sought analogies or highlighted the stark differences between later nineteenth century society and our own. These are not always helpful when responding to the text. What can be agreed is that the text does to varying extents engage with concerns regarding race, class and gender.

Biographical Contexts

We can begin with a biographical outline of key dates in a writer's life. Facts such as the dates of publication of particular works can provide some sense of the writer's literary development or changing concerns.

In the case of *Dracula*, a number of Stoker's biographical details have been considered significant by readers, including;
- The impact of Stoker's childhood illness and the influence of the myths and frightening stories his mother and nurse told to entertain him on his adult imagination.
- The tensions in his relationship with his friend and employer, Henry Irving, and Irving as a potential model for Dracula.
- Repressed and conservative elements of Stoker's sexuality.

Bram Stoker's Dracula: A Study Guide for A Level

Brief Biography of Abraham "Bram"' Stoker (1847-1912)

1847
Abraham Stoker born in Clontarf, Dublin on the 8th November, 1847. His father was a prominent civil servant, while his mother wrote and established charity work in the city. As a child, Stoker was bedridden with illness.

1864
Stoker begins his degree at Trinity College, Dublin. In spite of his prolonged childhood illness, he gains credit as a fine sportsman, particularly gifted at football.

1866
Stoker followed his father into the civil service and worked in administration at Dublin Castle for over a decade. He produced a manual while there - *The Duties of Clerks of Petty Sessions*. He also contributed to freelance journalism and theatre reviews to the *Dublin Mail*.

1876
Stoker is acquainted with leading literary circles in Dublin, including Oscar Wilde (Stoker will later marry Oscar Wilde's first significant love, Florence Balcombe). In 1876 Bram Stoker was introduced to famed actor Henry Irving, and would go on to forge a friendship and working partnership which would take him away from Ireland and the civil service.

1878
Stoker moves to London against family wishes. He begins his career as an actor-manager with the Lyceum Theatre, under the supervision of renowned actor Henry Irving.
On the 4th December 1878 he marries Florence Balcombe.

1879
Noel, the only child of Florence and Bram, is born.

1881
Stoker's first work of prose fiction *'Under the Sunset'* is published. He goes on to write numerous horror stories for magazines and 17 novels.

1890
Stoker's full-length novel, *The Snake's Pass*, is published.

1897
After at least five years of drafting, *Dracula* is published.

1912
Stoker wrote up until his death in 1912. Death was said to have been from exhaustion. Some critics suggested a link to tertiary syphilis, but this has since been contested as a misreading of the coroner's notes.
Despite its later fame, *Dracula* is not mentioned in Stoker's obituaries.

1914
Stoker's widow Florence publishes Stoker's posthumous collection *Dracula's Guest and Other Weird Stories*.

1922
An adaption of Dracula is produced on film as *'Nosferatu'*. Names of characters and some key aspects of the narrative differ. Florence sues the film makers for use of 'Dracula' without the estate's permission.

TASK: Exploring Biographical Contexts

Stoker presents his admiration of Henry Irving in *Personal Reminiscences of Henry Irving*, published in 1906. There is little doubt about how Stoker regarded his employer. He wrote in a tone akin to hero worship. Writing of their first meeting, Stoker records that;

"From that hour began a friendship as profound, as close, as lasting as can be between two men" (1: 33).

He states that *"I never found his appearance, bearing or manner other than the best"* (1: 260) and later passionately declares *"my love and admiration for Irving were such that nothing I could tell to others—nothing that I can recall to myself—could lessen his worth"* (2: 341).

Barbara Belford in Stoker's biography asserts "*Dracula* is all about Irving as the vampire".

As you read and explore *Dracula* consider to what extent you agree with the view expressed by in Belford's quote above?

You can explore in the following ways:

- Some critics have read the relationship between Harker and Dracula at the start of the novel to be a reflection of the unequal nature of the relationship between Stoker and Irving. While Stoker was full of praise for Irving, his employer was more reserved in his judgements. Can you find support in the text for the link Belford makes?
- Could an alternative link be made, for example, to the relationship portrayed between Jack Seward and Van Helsing?
- When you complete your study you may wish to revisit this question to see if you agree with your initial thoughts.

TASK: Stoker in his own words

Stoker wrote of his childhood illness: "*In my babyhood I used, I understand, to be often at the point of death. Certainly till I was about seven years old I never knew what it was to stand upright. This early weakness, however, passed away in time and I grew into a strong boy*"

Reminiscences 1: 31-32

To what extent might this experience have influenced Stoker's writing?

Can Stoker's journey from sickbed to health and strength be traced in any of the characters in the novel?

Limitations of biographical readings: Stoker's 'Monstrous sexuality'?

Over time, a number of academic responses have sought to establish a direct link between the fear of the monstrous predator in *Dracula* and the horror expressed across London society in response to Oscar Wilde's trial and imprisonment for sexual relations and blackmail of young males. The emerging scandal, prosecution and eventual imprisonment of Wilde took place between 1895-1897, originally believed to be the time Stoker wrote and re-drafted the novel.

Biographers have noted Stoker's strenuous and public disavowal of former acquaintance Wilde, alongside contemporary essays and communications, in which Stoker appeared to be expressing revulsion for any expression of sexuality deemed to be unconventional or abnormal.

This over time has been conflated with readings of his relationship with employer Irving as an obsession beyond platonic admiration. Stoker's communications with the poet Walt Whitman are often cited, as is the assertion that Florence and Stoker did not continue a physical relationship after the birth of their child, one year into their marriage in 1879.

An image of Florence Balcombe, drawn by Oscar Wilde

There is an implication that Stoker was struggling with aspects of his sexuality and that this struggle can be traced in the presentation of the predatory Dracula and his proprietal behaviour towards Jonathan Harker, whom he claims as *"mine"*.

Such readings suggest the novel is a direct response to anxieties Stoker felt regarding his own sexuality. Conversely, other biographers have repeated the assumption that the Stokers were not physically intimate and present a thesis that as a man of the theatre, Bram Stoker pursued physical relationships with women elsewhere and contracted a form of syphilis which contributed towards his death.

While biographical information can support exploration of a writer or a particular work, there are a number of difficulties with over-reliance on biographical conjecture when interpreting a text.

The supposition that *Dracula* enacts Stoker's struggle with latent homosexual thoughts not only relies on a belief that the novel was embarked upon in 1895, but also fails to recognise the strength and importance of homo-social bonds for Victorian gentlemen. Such camaraderie and mutual respect between men is portrayed in the continued collaboration of Holmwood, Morris and Seward after Lucy makes her marriage choice.

Some biographical readings also superimpose modern categories of sexual identity onto a Victorian text. In addition, the extensive drafting and research notes discovered now indicate *Dracula* was the product of years of drafting and revising from as early as 1890, pre-dating Wilde's trial.

The evaluation of the Stokers' marital relations relies on information passed down distant descendants. Even if true, the sense of spouses leading separate lives was not a rare occurrence for many upper and middle class unions, as these were often matches based on financial security and stability of future lineage.

A note of caution!

While there is certainly some support for interpretations of the novel as a presentation of the anxieties of late Victorian society regarding "monstrous" sexuality, it is another thing to assert authorial intention based on biography without providing substantial textual evidence. Throughout the guide, there will be further consideration of the presentation of sexuality in the text which does draw support from the language and imagery employed by Stoker. This should provide a note of caution that the reader should always seek to balance a consideration of the significance of wider contexts with a close reading of the text.

1.2 Historical Contexts; the *fin-de-siècle*

In this section we will;

- *Demonstrate understanding of the significance and influence of the contexts in which Dracula was written and received*
- *Explore connections across literary texts and contexts*
- *To consider wider social and historical contexts*

Victorian Britain

> **Fin de siècle**
>
> *A French term meaning the 'end of the century', or relating to this time. It is used in particular to describe the artistic, moral and social elements of the late nineteenth century.*

The nineteenth century saw a transition from traditional to technological innovation. The period is referred to as the Victorian age, delineated by Queen Victoria's reign from 1837-1901. The pace and encompassing nature of change to social, religious and economic practices generated a number of fears and anxieties in late Victorian society.

In the novel this can be seen in the tensions between science and superstition, the sense of outsider as other and the anxieties surrounding sexuality and gender. In the text Eastern European folklore is juxtaposed with industrialisation. Science was presented as a search for knowledge, replacing old belief systems. The growth of capitalism created an increased sense of isolation and alienation. The fear of reverse colonisation was a product of a declining Empire, as England saw threats from conflicts in Eastern Europe and the United States emerging as the supreme Western power in global trade.

The mid to late nineteenth century was an age of invention. In Victorian England, there was a firm belief that the developments in science and technology would enable the individual to better both self and environment. Institutional Christianity was questioned and newer sects and systems of belief emerged. In the arts, an evolution of the earlier Romantic emphasis on self, emotion and imagination combined with a neo-classical concept of public role of art and the social responsibility of the artist.

While the Victorian era encompasses a diverse range of writers, many literary works share the belief that literature could be used as a means of bridging a number of oppositions; self and society, personal and political, the subjective and objective. Literature became the public use of private experience. This may explain the rise of dramatic monologue, autobiography and autobiographical fiction at this time. Victorian literature attempts to combine individuality, originality, intensity and sincerity of writers with public accessibility and social relevance.

In the 1880s a severe economic depression had reduced Britain's power as the 'workshop of the world'. 1889 saw the London Dockers' Strike and Marxist parties began to appear in England as the growing professional middle class were drawn to socialist rather than liberal ideas.

Some critics, such as Robert *siècle*, highlight the parallels between Victorian England and the modern United States. He finds in both the

"same unblinking worship of independence and of hard cash; there was the same belief in institution, patriotism. democracy, individualism, organised religion, philanthropy, sexual morality, the family, capitalism, and progress".

Eagleton, in his *'Flight to the Real'* argues;

"For this above all is the age of artistic slumming, in which some raw, fascinating but fearful underworld lurks beneath the paper-thin structure of civilisation".

This approach was seen as preferable to a vacuous middle class society, built on crime, labour, money and filth, but desperate to hide its roots and deem itself cultured.

Dracula as 'invasion' text

Much of the horror of the text is linked to the idea of an invasion of the domestic setting. The genre of the text can be seen as supernatural or 'uncanny'. Looking at Freud's later definition of uncanny it is worth noting the German term used, *'unheimlich'* which translates 'unhomely'. The undead are beyond the familiar or homely as being simultaneously alive and dead but there is also a sense of the women in the text subverting expectations of the domestic sphere. Lucy transforms not only into the undead, but is described as wanton and voluptuous. A wider Victorian concern linked to the anxieties in defining normal and abnormal behaviour. Oscar Wilde's trial drew attention as some felt masculinity under threat, while doctors were often called upon to identify and categorise abnormal or pathological behaviour.

Previous vampiric texts such as George McDonald's *Lilith* (1895) were set in a timeless Christian past, with links to possession and witchcraft; Stoker's vampire is a modern threat, and while there is still a spiritual aspect to Van Helsing's methods, he supports his actions with a proposed medical model.

In this, Stoker may be referencing the contemporary use of vampirism as a metaphor or trope for disease, specifically syphilis. Stoker himself was rumoured to have contracted tertiary syphilis. The Contagious Diseases Act had been passed in 1886, as a response to the belief that prostitutes had spread sexually transmitted diseases and were therefore weakening the British fighting forces. In addition to holding vulnerable women responsible for the spread of disease, the act enabled examination of any woman suspected of being a prostitute. As blood tests were not developed until 1906, decisions were made about whether a woman was infected or cured purely based on what a doctor could see.

Likewise, in the text Van Helsing and the others look for visible symptoms that the women have been infected, noting teeth, colour of lips, pallor and any emaciation. Mina is 'marked' as unclean suggesting it is an infection of body rather than soul. There are two doctors presented in *Dracula* and they would seem to claim their professional control as a control over women. Van Helsing's transfusions and later aggressive solution for Lucy's infection creates anxieties similar to those felt by the general public in the face of the development of invasive medical surgery, which seemed to violate in order to cure.

The medical model can also be seen as a metaphor for the impact on society and community. Dracula's victims become social lepers, and for both Mina and Lucy individual fate is seen as less important as the danger which they may pose to the social group once infected by the vampire.

Some critics have seen Dracula himself as an allegory for the threat of disease. Popular Victorian belief was that VD (now STDs) originated abroad and Dracula has also come from a foreign space. The fear of the outsider linked to fear of degeneration and dilution of blood, where blood was seen as symbolising race or purity. These ideas were presented in Max Nordau's text *Degeneration* in 1895, and later used by Lombroso in earlier criminology to identify physical characteristics which may correlate with criminal behaviour. Mina references to both Nordau and Lombroso in her discussion of Dracula's '*child brain*'.

Lombroso, with images of skulls and photographs of men considered to have 'criminal' faces.

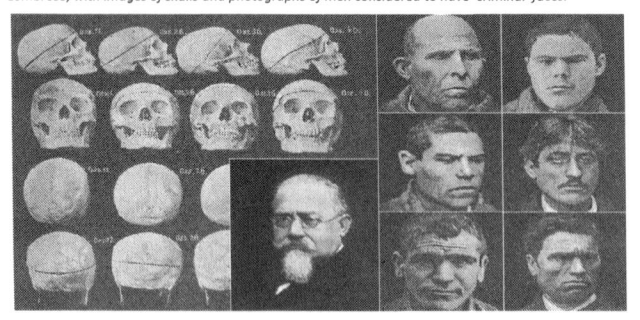

The Whitechapel Vampire

Some have drawn attention to the potential overlap between the time frame of *Dracula* and the notorious 'Jack the Ripper' murders. Stoker was more than conscious of these, as the Lyceum Theatre where he worked as manager had been encouraged to shut down a production of *Dr Jekyll and Mr Hyde* for fear it would encourage copycats, or allow the culprit to move through the busy theatre crowds.

Stoker's notes suggest that he began formulating drafts of *Dracula* as early as 1890. There is some support for the possibility that the Ripper case did influence the creation of a monster terrorising London's streets, as some of the contemporary news reporting illustrates.

The *Daily Telegraph* labelled insane criminals as *'vampires, of whom society has the right to be quickly rid, without too much attention to the theories of mental experts'* (10 September 1888). A week later, London pamphlets decried that the man scourging Whitechapel *'puts all the vampire stories of fiction to bed'*.

An extended front page article appeared in the *East London Advertiser* on the 6th October 1888. Its title was *'A Thirst for Blood'* as it argued that the crimes are so disgusting and horrific that *'the myths of the Dark Ages arise before the imagination. Ghouls, vampires, bloodsuckers...take form'*.

The text itself places at least two of Dracula's London properties in or around the Whitechapel area, with references to streets which ran close to locations where victims were discovered. Jonathan Harker interviews one of Dracula's workmen:

> ...he gave me the destinations of the boxes. There were, he said, six in the cartload which he took from Carfax and left at 197 Chicksand Street, Mile End New Town, and another six which he deposited at Jamaica Lane, Bermondsey. If then the Count meant to scatter these ghastly refuges of his over London, these places were chosen as the first of delivery, so that later he might distribute more fully. The systematic manner in which this was done made me think that he could not mean to confine himself to two sides of London. He was now fixed on the far east of the northern shore, on the east of the southern shore, and on the south...

Monstrous feminity

Dracula would seem to attack the weakest within the domestic sphere, with any physical, moral or spiritual weakness placing a person in danger. Urban women in particular were seen as lacking social and sexual control. These fears in turn were linked to their role as child-bearers. They were not believed to be responsible for defending 'purity' of nation. Stoker can be seen to exaggerate this idea with his subversion of the mother and child. In the novel, women are made monstrous as they feed on children. Lucy is lost and this is indicated in her callous treatment of the child. Mina is ultimately saved at the close of the novel when she embraces her 'proper' role as mother.

The female vampire was a symbol of the monstrous threat to Victorian masculinity;

"the product of the disruption of perceived gender hierarchies, a horsewomen of the Victorian apocalypse who threatens the end of the 'race' and the slow death of the British Empire on its throne".

In the next section, the social construct of the 'New Woman' will be considered.

Bram Stoker's Dracula: A Study Guide for A Level

1.3 Social Contexts: The 'New Woman'

In this section we will;

- *Demonstrate understanding of the significance and influence of the contexts in which Dracula was written and received*
- *Explore connections across literary texts and contexts*
- *To consider wider social and historical contexts*

Sexual Politics: The 'New Woman'?

Victorian society was very much concerned with the rise of independent and liberal-thinking women. There were anxieties about sexuality, particularly relating to men abandoning traditional masculinity, with the 1889 Cleveland Street revealing the friends and son of the Prince of Wales had been using a homosexual brothel and 1895 dominated by the public trial and humiliation of Oscar Wilde, an acquaintance of Stoker, who had visited the Wilde home in Dublin over a number of years. The social fears related to the blurring of sexual boundaries.

The century saw reforms to marriage and divorce laws, such as the 1857 Married Women's Property Bill. This was challenged as there was a fear it may give women 'citizenship'.

The New Woman was educated and wished for entry into the professions. She worked outside of the house. This was a middle-class concern, as the lower classes had often worked through necessity. To men, a woman denying their traditional role was a denial of womanhood.

The Conservative writer Mrs Eliza Lynn Linton saw New Women "*as modern man haters 'unsexed by the atrophy of their instincts'*", while Grant Allen in portrayal of a liberated woman as a champion of free love in *The Woman Who Did*. The contribution of some female artists to the decadent *'Yellow Book'* reinforced the association of the New Woman with immorality in the public mind.

The social purity movement of the 1880s was built on the fear of women as independent sexual subjects. There was enforcement of conformity, as in 1877 with Annie Besant and the obscenity trial (she had co-produced a text on family planning). The birth prevention organization was founded out of this. Pseudo-scientific and medical accounts of 'unnatural' behaviour lead to labels of sado-masochism, nymphomania and inversion. There was the concept of a predatory woman, building on the nineteenth century fear of excess and undisciplined sexuality.

Cartoons depicted the New Woman as mannish in dress and appetites, as in the *Punch* cartoon below; "*Laughter often concealed real fears or the danger posed by advanced or independent womanhood to the status quo*".

Gertrude. "MY DEAR JESSIE, WHAT ON EARTH IS THAT BICYCLE SUIT FOR?"
Jessie. "WHY, TO WEAR, OF COURSE." *Gertrude.* "BUT YOU HAVEN'T GOT A BICYCLE!"
Jessie. "NO; BUT I'VE GOT A SEWING MACHINE!"

Bram Stoker's Dracula: A Study Guide for A Level

Society would criticise the independent middle-class woman as a type of 'Fallen Woman', highlighting class concerns. There are links to social aspirations: *"a partial, ambiguous criticism not only of society's double standards, but also of aristocratic attitudes"*. Mina follows this arc when she declares herself 'Unclean!' after Dracula's attack.

New Woman as Monster

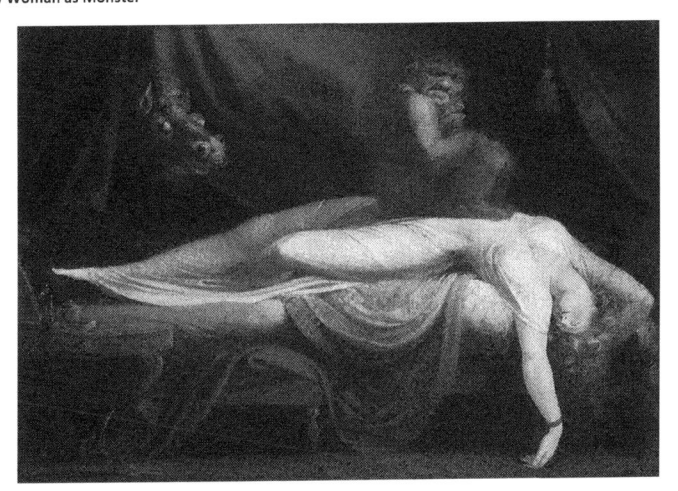

TASK: New Woman as Monster

The painting above, *The Nightmare* by Henry Fuseli, was painted in 1781. It shows an incubus – a male demon or sexual predator - crushing the torso of a woman in a deep sleep, while a dark horse, symbolic of nightmares, can be seen.

The female is draped in white and is in a passive, vulnerable position. This could be seen as the traditional artistic representation of the female as victim.

Now look at the image overleaf. It was produced by Philip Burne-Jones in 1897.
It is titled *'The Vampire'*.

- What are the main differences between each of these images?
- What is this suggesting about society's changing view of women?
- How are these views presented in the novel *Dracula*?

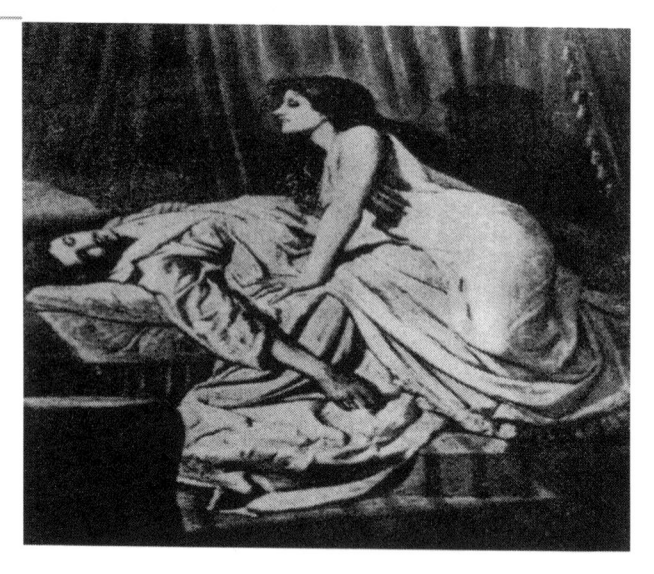

Scapegoating and the New Woman

Key term: psychomachia

The eternal struggle between good and evil where evil is defeated

Anthropologists such as Mary Douglas have noted that pollution fears and accusations of witchcraft share characteristics across place and time. The use of the idiom 'witch-hunt' draws on this - many felt Wilde for example became a scapegoat for the general distrust of 'dandies' and men engaged in conspicuous consumption of fashion or luxury goods. Society seeks to view the universe as dualistic. Clear boundaries separate a group from danger or foreignness. Simplistic notions of purity inside a group against the evil outside are promoted to maintain group identity and security. Northop Frye notes the concept of *psychomachia* - the eternal struggle between good and evil where evil is defeated.

Victorians tentatively accepted the model of outsider pollution. There were pressures to conform while the model was losing its clarity. The struggle to maintain power can create scapegoats. Whole social groups such as the Jewish community or individuals such as Wilde can be used as scapegoats for social problems. Women were also the target of moral campaigns.

It is useful to look at scape-goating or the use of ritual victim in *Dracula*. Lucy Westenra has to be sacrificed to restore lost order. The scapegoat should be of the community, although marginal. Initially, Lucy seems an unlikely scapegoat.

She is young, beautiful and virtuous. However, it can be argued that as her father is dead her social links are tenuous. Hers is potentially a flawed rather than controlled sexuality, as in her flippant comment on marrying all three suitors. Sleepwalking as a state had been traditionally linked with potential moral looseness as it was a lack of control of the body. She is also unconscious when she yields to Dracula - it could be argued that this removes responsibility although the scapegoat model would perhaps suggest that her lack of control is a lack of true virtue.

By contrast, the men are controlled in their competition and seen to calmly accept her final choice of husband. There is a potential source of violence which ultimately is turned towards the un-dead Lucy. This violent sacrifice returns Lucy to purity and the possibility of eternal salvation. The act of staking is presented as religious and communal. In confronting Lucy, the men purge their fear of female sexuality and also their own desires.

TASK: Exploring Contexts: Representations of Gender and Sexuality

Evaluate the ways in which *Dracula* provides commentary on women in Victorian society.

You could consider:

- The representation of women and sexuality
- References to power in the text
- The language and imagery used to present Lucy, Mina and the female vampires.

1.4 Literary Contexts: Urban and Imperial Gothic

In this section we will;
- *Demonstrate understanding of the significance and influence of the contexts in which Dracula was written and received*
- *Explore connections across literary texts and contexts*
- *To consider wider social and historical contexts*

The Novel at the *Fin-de-Siècle*

As the nineteenth century drew to a close, philosophical certainties taken as absolutes were changing. Instability of gender roles became evident in the moral panics surrounding the emergence of the 'New Woman', the decadent and the dandy. There was further economic instability in society coupled with the rise of trade unionism and colonial rebellion. London may have been a centre for global capital, but was in a heightened state of tension due to the emerging signs of urban poverty and homelessness.

Living conditions in the Seven Dials slum, London. *'Seven Dials'* by Gustav Dore (1872)

Sally Ledger (1995) proposes that the lack of certainty was reflected in the form of the novel. The 'three decker' gave way to single volume novels and novellas. There was less reliance on omniscient narrators. While Gothic literature traditionally had stories and multiple narrators, these had usually worked round to full exploration. Fin de siècle texts presented gaps and puzzles, as *"the reader was no longer given the security of an assured interpretation"* (Ledger, 1995).

> *"The cultural transformations of the vampire that take place during the course of the nineteenth century are closely linked to the developing discourses of the period, principally gender, disease and the decline of the Imperial (that is to say, British) race. There are links to degeneration and the myths relating to "feared collapse of gender categories, the location of syphilitic infection in the female body and the health of the Empire".*
>
> **Alexandra Warwick Vampires and the Empire: Fears and Fictions of the 1890s**

'Fantastic' Fiction: Urban Gothic

The Romance revival in the final two decades of the nineteenth century saw the rise of the genre known as 'the fantastic'.

The fictional world is often based on a model of the world which is mimetic. This is 'violently breached' by fantastic, changed into one where fantastic does not violate laws of reality:

- The impossible event must genuinely be happening, not a dream or hallucination.
- There should be a tone of initial disbelief and horror.
- The text should emphasise the violation and transgression of expectations, as when Dracula is seen in Piccadilly at noon.

The Fantastic contravenes the realist mode but it is very much a modern genre. If we compare to medieval or Renaissance texts, it was possible for a knight to encounter a dragon, yet there was no sense that the supernatural violated the sense of the world.

Initially writers set narratives in 'exotic' settings known for superstition and folklore. Spain and Italy were popular locations. Writers such as Radcliffe exploited such settings but ensured by the end of the text a rational explanation was provided for 'supernatural' events.

With the exception of the ghost story, the fantastic text of the later nineteenth century insists on a modern setting that the reader can identify with. These were often urban locations. Science was presented, along with a discourse based on empiricism to support descriptions and explanations of supernatural phenomena.

It can be useful to think of this style as 'Urban Gothic'. The wider Romance revival was a reaction to high realism of 1870s. Writers of the 1880s attacked 'character' novels. Naturalist novels tried to introduce poor or criminal individuals to the middle-class readers. There was no longer room for divine Providence as presented in works by writers such as Zola. The public rejected this style and called for healthy English fiction.

In the early 1890s there was an appetite for bold adventures. Writers such as Stevenson, Kipling, Haggard, Conan Doyle and H G Wells used information about countries in the Empire and new belief systems to make stories interesting and exotic. Alongside the taste for adventure and exoticism, there was an opposing focus on domestic purity and preserving boundaries. There was a wish to stabilize distinctions and ways of categorising the world.

Nationalism was sited in two areas, the personal and familial, and the mass ritual of sport, politics or group congregation. The middle classes relied on these two elements to determine own selfhood. Fears about devolution and degeneracy had developed in response to Darwin's model of evolution and survival of the fittest. Criminals were seen as related to primitive ancestors and somehow less evolved that the moral citizen.

Recruiters had already noted frail and sickly recruits in the East End of London. Women were often treated as inferior or infantile species. They were granted a certain type of strength, as evidenced in the idealised woman presented in Patmore's poem *Angel in the House*, which presented the domestic role as crucial, as the woman was needed "to save Man from his own baser instincts and lead him toward Heaven". The roles of wife and mother were deified, becoming a domestic religion.

Further Reading: For more on Victorian Urban Gothic, see Kathleen L Spencer *Purity and Danger: Dracula, the Urban Gothic and the Late Victorian Degeneracy Crisis*

The Imperial Gothic

Dracula was published in 1897. This period was termed the *'fin-de-siècle'* and the text is seen as an example of the 'Imperial Gothic'. At this time "*Gothic represented excess and exaggeration, the product of the wild and uncivilised, a world that constantly tended to overflow cultural boundaries.*" (Punter).

London was the seat of British modernity and imperialistic power. It was the centre of banking and a source of investment capital. Dracula is a threat to this power, with his ability to assimilate and conquer. Britain believed it had a 'civilising mission' and sought to impose racial and moral beliefs on other nationalities. An example is seen early in the text, when Harker comments on the Szgany people, deeming them "*outside all Law...fearless and without religion, save superstition, and they take only their own varieties of the Romany tongue*". Harker is fascinated but condescending.

Dracula as a keen student of English history and customs recognised these differences in perspectives, and in celebrating his own heritage when he warns Jonathan Harker "*our ways are not your ways*". Stoker made a deliberate choice to site Dracula's castle in the Carpathian Mountains, in an area known for unrest and proxy conflicts. Romania and Transylvania were populated with multiple ethnic groups. In the Victorian era, diversity was seen as instability. There is a fear that Dracula will import this instability on reaching England and there is a fear of social dissolution.

Dracula's desire to assimilate into English society and pass as a local is an example of reverse colonisation. In British minds, this ability to gain power was a revolt of the inferior. Dracula has a keen intelligence and has studied English history, geography, politics, economics, law and national customs. Nevertheless, he does not see his approach as a degeneration of his own race, proudly telling Harker of his Eastern European routes and history of warfare.

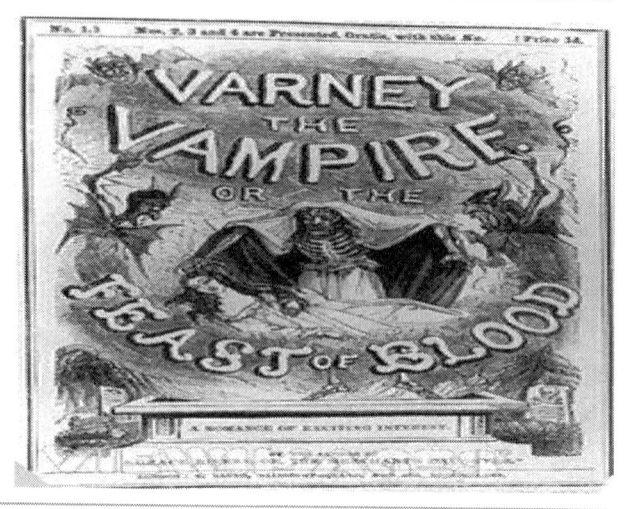

Gender and Infection

Dracula was published in 1897, the year of Queen Victoria's Diamond Jubilee. In earlier texts, the vampire was male, while in *Dracula* all vampires bar Dracula are female. Earlier vampire fiction cast women as victims who would die or be in disgrace, not transform. Polodori's *The Vampyre*, written at the start of the century, presents the vampire as an aristocratic murderer and the later penny dreadful series *Varney the Vampire* in the 1840s sees vampires in the guise of serial killers. The victims in these texts were vulnerable women, often orphans or lacking a male patriarchal figure.

The trope of infection is a much later addition and one that is explored by Stoker. It has been noted that as the century draws to a close "*the figure of the vampire acquires an immoral aspect in addition to its supernatural, it becomes one of the vital components...the female body that is increasingly seen as the source of danger, and the disruption of gender identity as one of the effects of contagion*".

Men are also infected or emasculated on contact with the vampire. While it is often indirect contact, they become like women. In the interaction between Harker and the female vampires they are presented as dreadful due to the unstable gender traits. They enact an assault on the submissive Harker.

In the text when a woman becomes masculine the punishment is severe. Once Lucy has been contaminated and after death exhibits unhealthy appetites she is aggressively staked. It can be noted that Dracula is merely stabbed. The stake recalls the medieval lance and as such the group of men can be seen to desecrate her as earlier forms of pillage, even in the act of saving her. In public life, the vampire was used as a metaphor for the pollution created by syphilis, which was very much seen as the responsibility of prostitutes, infecting the nation with disease. Even in this text while claiming to defend purity and save women from becoming victims, the men distrust and fear Mina and Lucy at various points.

In Sheridan Le Fanu's *Carmilla* (1871) - an influence on Stoker - it is women who threaten women. The text has a number of women but lacks a maternal figure. It shares with Dracula a sense that the victim is somewhat complicit in their fate - Lucy's sleepwalking is a freedom of movement which can be linked to freedom of morals in the Victorian mind.

Science versus the supernatural

Another key characteristic of the Imperial Gothic style is the structuring of binary oppositions in texts between empirical science, seen to represent rational thinking, and traditional religion and belief systems, which rely on faith in the supernatural.

Science is placed in opposition to superstition and folklore. Seward is a disciple of reason and applies empirical scientific methods to his thinking. Van Helsing is also a practitioner of empirical science but is open to applying remedies based on superstitions. In a text celebrating empirical reasoning there is some irony that it is Doctor Seward who cannot fathom the mystery of Lucy's illness.

Van Helsing is highly educated, recognised as "*MD, Dph, D Lit, etc., etc.*" and seems technologically aware. He has been a mentor for Seward. Ultimately it is a combination of medicine and folklore which help confront Dracula. He gently criticises Seward for failing to have an open mind, noticing "t*hat which is outside of your daily life is not of account to you*".

Van Helsing has some similarities to Dracula. Neither man is a native speaker; both prove there is some truth in superstition. Van Helsing is still a representative of the "Other" but serves to resolve tensions, becoming a mediator between the tensions of East and West.

TASK: Belief Systems, Science and Superstition in *Dracula*

Create a table using heading as in the example below. As you read, note the beliefs expressed by Van Helsing and Seward in the novel.

These can be:
- Religious beliefs
- Scientific beliefs
- Superstitions.

	Seward	Van Helsing
Personal religious beliefs		
Beliefs relating to vampires		
Beliefs relating to the afterlife (e.g. Lucy as 'undead')		
Superstitions		

TASK: Exploring Wider Contexts

Make sure you have read the novel before attempting this task. Aim to respond to each heading with an extended paragraph, making one essay-style response.

Discuss the presentation of key social and historical contexts in the novel.

Historical Contexts

- What does the novel tell us life in 1890s Britain?

Cultural Contexts
- How is 'culture' referenced in the novel?
- How are knowledge and education presented or treated in the narrative?
- To what extent does culture influence the social order and individual sensibility?

Gender and Sexuality
- How are males and females presented in the novel?
- Are certain behaviours or roles presented as masculine and feminine?
- Does the text challenge or subvert conventional gender stereotypes?
- In what ways does gender impact upon experiences within the narrative?

Power
- What power relationships and power struggles are represented?
- How is the relationship between social classes and the social hierarchy explored?

Race
- Are issues of race addressed in the novel?
- Does the narrative voice challenge or support representations of race?

Religion
- What part does religion play in the narrative?
- Are there a range of belief systems presented in the text?

Exploring Wider Contexts: A scene of Victorian London (*Aldgate*, Gustav Dore)

Part Two: Introducing Critical Approaches

Part Two:
Introducing Critical Approaches

2.1 *Narrative Overview and Structure*
2.2 *Characterisation*
2.3 *Themes and Symbolism*
2.4 *Settings: Crossing Boundaries*
2.5 *The 'Other'*

2.1 Narrative and Structure

In this section we will;

- *Develop informed responses to Dracula, using associated concepts and terminology*
- *Analyse ways in which meanings are shaped in texts*
- *Explore literary texts informed by different interpretations*

Narrative Overview

When responding to *Dracula*, you should consider how the writer's linguistic and literary techniques enhance or develop themes and characterisation, and how they contribute to the overall narrative style.

The novel is divided into 27 chapters. The narrative is not linear although it is broadly chronological. There is use of interlacing narrative to provide information from various perspectives.

It begins with the records kept in Jonathan Harker's journal of his business trip to Transylvania, in order to finalise a property transaction with Dracula. Journal entries run across chapters, at times suggesting a significant development has taken place within the matter of a few hours. This follows the conventions of the newly emerging detective fiction. Stoker himself cited the influence of Wilkie Collins and *The Woman in White*, which can be seen in the use of the framing device and epistolary style.

The narrative can be found to divide into key strands. It begins with the strange encounters Harker has with his client Dracula and his perilous escape, before returning to England, where the parallel narratives of Seward's case study of his patient Renfield and the mysterious illness affecting Lucy Westenra following her sleepwalking in Whitby.

After the fantastic horror of ridding the deceased Lucy of her vampire curse, a significant portion of the narrative is given to the drawing together in a common cause, as Mina and Jonathan join Van Helsing and Lucy's former suitors to confront and defeat the common enemy Dracula. Renfield's descent into madness would appear as a subplot, but is revealed as having a direct link to Dracula's intentions.

The pursuit of Dracula across Europe builds to a climax, with the added peril of Mina's imminent transformation into an un-dead vampire. Some critics have found the final conquest of Dracula itself to be quite rapid and anti-climactic.

An epilogue is provided in the form of Jonathan's postscript note; where he details how the surviving younger men have gone on to marry, while he and Mina happily have a son, now sitting on Van Helsing's knee. The conclusion has Jonathan note the incredible nature of the tale recorded, and how on reflection, it seems to lack any concrete evidence to support the existence of evil and supernatural elements.

> **TASK: Structural Choices**
>
> What are the effects of drawing on a range of sources and perspectives?
>
> What is the effect of breaks in chronology, or the representation of the same event from a different character's viewpoint?

Narrative methods: *Dracula* as Polyphonic Text

The series of first person narratives provide immediacy and increase the reader's sense of horror and bewilderment; the absence of a dominant voice denies the reader certainty about the reliability of the account.

Throughout the text, the reliability of the point of view being presented must be evaluated. It could be argued that this makes the text more democratic, as it is not privileging a single viewpoint. In this way Dracula could be seen as an example of Bakhtin's polyphonic text.

> **Bakhtin (1981) Novel as Dialogic or Polyphonic Text**
>
> *Bakhtin sees language "as essentially dialogic; it takes place in a social context".*
>
> *For him, any word "is directly, blatantly oriented towards a future answer word". He does not find genre a useful way of responding to literary texts. The insistence of categorising deems a text monologic in world view and ideology, suggesting there is one way to interpret it.*
>
> *For Bahktin, the novel is a dialogic or polyphonic text. He borrows the term 'polyphonic' from musical analysis and sees it as a useful term for the way in which a novel can allow "a number of diverse voices to interact".*
>
> *Even when a text makes use of a third person narrator, Bakhtin argues that the use of free indirect speech and an implicit reader "embody awareness of its place in an orchestra of different voices with their varied points of view". There is such an orchestra in Dracula, both in voices and media used.*

In *Dracula*, large sections of the text are presented through the records of Harker, Seward and Mina, and there are further contributions from Lucy, Van Helsing, Holmwood and Quincey, as well as other minor characters. A range of texts including cuttings from newspapers and the ship's log provide additional information of events beyond the immediate experiences of the participating characters.

Van Helsing aside, the main voices of the text are relatively youthful and inexperienced. One criticism levelled at Stoker's style has noted that there is perhaps not enough differentiation between voices and professions of these characters. A counter-argument sees the relatively similarity in social class and register as part of Stoker's design and it has been suggested that;

"by maintaining a constancy of style throughout and emphasising the beliefs which they hold in common, Stoker further diminishes any individualising traits. The narrators appear to speak with one voice" Carol Senf,1997)

The main narrators are English and drawn from the emerging middle class. There is some uniformity of voice, particularly the register employed by Seward and Harker as two young professionals. It may also be argued that there is very little to distinguish the aristocratic voices of Lord Goldaming and Holmwood.

It can be argued that Lucy and Mina do diverge, and the content of the exchange of letters gives an indication of the differences in lifestyle, expectations and values held by each due to the conditions they have experienced.

Quincey Morris is also presented with a degree of difference, although as an American character he remains on the periphery and has little influence on the narrative, despite losing his life in the final battle against Dracula.

Throughout, Dracula remains the object of investigation. There is some reported speech in the opening chapters presenting Jonathan's journal of the visit to the castle but beyond this his voice is seldom heard.

Van Helsing is crucial to the action and provides an interpretation of the uncanny events, yet has a limited role as narrator. He has no journal or record, with his views often presented embedded in the records of other characters. When his views are reported, they are rendered with strange and inconsistent speech idioms as a marker of his European roots. The one direct entry he is allowed is recorded using Seward's preferred medium of the phonograph.

TASK: Exploring the text

Compare Van Helsing's final memorandum in Chapter 27 with Harker's earlier account of the three female vampires.

Both accounts share a sense of fascination with these women. There is a refraction of Harker's description with an acknowledgement that these were *"the same three women that Harker saw..."* Unlike Harker, he states the power of the fascination but is able to take control and stake the women. Critics have argued that the staking is symbolic of sexual penetration and suggests the virility that the younger male characters are lacking.

Van Helsing is susceptible to the fascination but is more able to accept his feelings than Harker. He can recognise this may be shameful and wrong without being paralysed by fear or shame. Both men draw comparisons, contrasting *"the voluptuous vampires with the virtuous Mina"*. Both draw strange comfort from this, reinforcing Mina's function as the approved form of womanhood.

There is an interesting inversion of physical evaluation as at the point in the narrative where Dracula has potentially infected Mina, Mina's pale and ill demeanour is morally more acceptable that the *"fresh horror of that ruddy vampire sleep"*(Chapter 27). Her terror brings the group comfort in that it demonstrates she has not succumbed as Lucy did. She is not without power - her woeful voice seems mystical and is a voice of monition or warning that serves to rouse Van Helsing from a hypnotic state and into action.

While not given full voice, Van Helsing is nevertheless an active agent, with *"aggression overcoming fascination"* in contrast to the apparent inertia of Jonathan when in proximity to the vampires.

The epistolary novel and *Dracula*

The epistolary novel was traditionally a narrative presented as a series of letters, drawing from the term epistle. In literature a text is considered to be epistolary in structure if presented through a series of documents, which may be letters, but also diary entries, newspaper clippings and other recognisable texts. Earlier forms of this structure were often monologic, presenting the letters or journals of a single character, or dialogic, presenting an exchange of letters between two characters. Dracula can be seen as a polylogic text as a number of characters present written and recorded accounts of the events.

Epistolary Structure of *Dracula* (1897 edition)

The monologic perspective of Jonathan's account of his extraordinary experiences at Dracula's castle gives way to the polyphonic voices of the text, alternating between the social and personal communications of the letters and the professional register of Dr Seward's recorded observations. The text is also made up of other documentary evidence such as telegrams, newspaper articles, ship logs, legal communications and memos. The table below lists the order and range of texts presented within the novel.

Chapter/ Month	
	Opening Note - Preface refers to 'papers' collected
Chapter 1 May	Jonathan Harker's journal, originally kept in shorthand
Chapter 2	Jonathan Harker's journal, originally kept in shorthand
Chapter 3	Jonathan Harker's journal, originally kept in shorthand
Chapter 4	Jonathan Harker's journal, originally kept in shorthand
Chapter 5 May	Letter from Mina Murray to Miss Lucy Westenra Letter from Lucy Westenra to Mina Murray Further letter from Mina Murray to Lucy Westenra Dr John Seward's diary (recorded on phonograph) Letter from Quincy P Morris to Hon. Arthur Holmwood Telegram from Arthur Holmwood to Quincey P Morris
Chapter 6 July	Mina Murray's Journal (Whitby) Dr Seward's Diary Mina Murray's Journal
Chapter 7 August	Newspaper cutting from *The Dailygraph,* pasted in Mina's journal Correspondent report, Whitby Log of The Demeter - voyage from Varna to Whitby Mina Murray's journal
Chapter 8 August	Mina Murray's journal Legal communication from Whitby to Messrs. Carter, Peterson & Co, London - an invoice of goods for boxes sent to Carfax Abbey Letter from Carter, Peterson & Co, to Billington & Son, Whitby Mina Murray's Journal 18th August Letter from Sister Agatha, Hospital of St Joseph and the Virgin Mary, Budapesth to Miss Wilhemina Murray 12th August Dr Seward's Diary reporting on Renfield
Chapter 9 Late August/ Early September	Letter Mina Harker to Lucy Westenra 24th August Letter from Lucy to Mina 30th August Dr Seward's Diary 20th August Lucy Westenra's Diary Letter from Arthur Holmwood to Dr Seward Telegram Arthur Holmwood to Dr Seward Letter Dr Seward to Arthur Holmwood Letter Van Helsing to Dr Seward Letter Dr Seward to Arthur Holmwood Dr Seward's Diary

	Telegram dated 4th September Dr Seward, London to Van Helsing, Amsterdam Telegram dated 5th September Dr Seward, London to Van Helsing, Amsterdam Telegram dated 6th September Dr Seward, London to Van Helsing, Amsterdam
Chapter 10 September	Letter Dr Seward to Hon Arthur Holmwood Dr Seward's diary Lucy Westenra's Diary Dr Seward's Diary
Chapter 11 September	Lucy Westenra's Diary 12th September Dr Seward's Diary 13th September Lucy Westenra's Diary 17th September Newspaper cutting from *Pall Mall Gazette* 18th September Dr Seward's Diary Telegram Van Helsing, Antwerp to Dr Seward, Carfax Dr Seward's Diary 18th September Memorandum left by Lucy Westenra 17th September
Chapter 12 September	Dr Seward's Diary 18/19th September Letter Mina Harker to Lucy Westenra (unopened) 17th September Coroner's Report from Patrick Hennessey MD Letter Mina Harker to Lucy Westenra (unopened) 18th September Dr Seward's Diary
Chapter 13 September	Dr Seward's Diary Mina Harker's Journal 22nd September, on train to Exeter Dr Seward's Diary 22nd September 'A Hampstead Mystery', article from *The Westminster Gazette* 25th September *The Westminster Gazette* Extra 25th September - 'The Bloofer Lady''
Chapter 14 September	Mina Harker's Journal Letter from Van Helsing to Mrs Mina Harker 24th September Telegram Mrs Harker to Van Helsing Mina Harker's Journal Letter Van Helsing to Mrs Harker 25th September 6 o'clock Letter Mrs Mina Harker to Van Helsing Jonathan Harker's Journal 26th September Dr Seward's Diary
Chapter 15 September	Dr Seward's Diary continued Note left by Van Helsing in hotel portmanteau directed to John Seward MD (undelivered) Dr Seward's Diary
Chapter 16 September	Dr Seward's Diary
Chapter 17 September	Dr Seward's Diary Mina Harker's Journal 29th September Dr Seward's Diary 29th September Mina Harker's Journal additional entry 29th September Dr Seward's Diary 30th September

	Jonathan Harker's Journal 29/30th September
	Mina Harker's Journal
Chapter 18 September/ October	Dr Seward's Diary 30th September continued
	Mina Harker's Journal 30th September
	Dr Seward's Diary 1st October
Chapter 19 October	Jonathan Harker's Journal 1st October 5.00am
	Dr Seward's Diary 1st October continued
	Mina Harker's Journal 1st/2nd October
Chapter 20 October	Jonathan Harker's Journal, evening of 1st October/ 2nd October
	Dr Seward's Diary 1st October
	Letter from Mitchell, Sons & Candy for Lord Godalming (Arthur Holmwood)
	Dr Seward's Diary 2nd October
Chapter 21 October	Dr Seward's Diary 3rd October
Chapter 22 October	Jonathan Harker's Journal 3rd October
Chapter 23 October	Dr Seward's Diary 3rd October
	Jonathan Harker's Journal 3rd/4th October
Chapter 24 October	Dr Seward's Phonograph Diary, recording spoken by Van Helsing for Jonathan Harker
	Jonathan Harker's Journal 4th October
	Mina Harker's Journal 5th October 5.00pm
	Dr Seward's Diary 5th October
	Jonathan Harker's Journal 5th October
Chapter 25 October	Dr Seward's Diary 11th October Evening
	Jonathan Harker's Journal 15th October Varna/ 17th October
	Telegram Lloyds of London to Lord Godalming
	Dr Seward's Diary 25-28th October
Chapter 26 October/ November	Dr Seward's Diary 29th October, handwritten on Varna train 30th October
	Mina Harker's Journal 30th October
	Jonathan Harker's Journal 30th October
	Mina Harker's Journal 30th October Evening
	Mina Harker's Memorandum, entered in journal
	Mina Harker's Journal
	Jonathan Harker's Journal 30th October night and 31st October
	Dr Seward's Diary 2nd November
	Mina Harker's Journal 31st October
Chapter 27 November	Mina Harker's Journal 2nd November
	Memorandum by Abraham van Helsing 4th November/ 5th November
	Jonathan Harker's Journal 4th November evening
	Dr Seward's Diary 4th/5th November
	Dr Van Helsing's Memorandum 5th November, afternoon
	Mina Harker's Journal 6th November
End Note	End-Note/ Postscript signed Jonathan Harker

2.2 Characterisation

In this section we will;
- *Develop informed responses to Dracula, using associated concepts and terminology*
- *Analyse ways in which meanings are shaped in texts*
- *Explore literary texts informed by different interpretations*

Exploring the character of Dracula

While he is the eponymous character of the novel, the Transylvanian noble Count Dracula does not directly present his own perspective or voice. Instead, the reader learns about his appearance, attitudes, powers and vulnerabilities through the records and journals kept by other characters.

When Jonathan Harker travels to Dracula's stately castle to finalise a property sale, he finds the Count a proud aristocrat who is keen to share his family history. Dracula is initially welcoming to Jonathan, and seems keen to learn as much as he can about English customs, language and history. He is well-spoken and intelligent in discussions. Dracula expresses an interest in the British Empire, and admires models of domination and control. He himself maintains power through capital. Gold is found in both the castle and Dracula's London home.

Bran Castle, believed to have inspired Dracula's Castle

Dracula reveals a contrasting side of his personality when Jonathan wanders into forbidden rooms within the castle and encounters three mysterious women. Dracula erupts in furious anger and violently casts the women away. It becomes clear that he is only interested in keeping Jonathan alive long enough to learn to fit in to English society. Dracula is intelligent in his manipulation and planning, stealing Jonathan's outfit to use when abducting village children in order to shift the blame. He takes pleasure in torturing Jonathan, inviting him to leave the castle before revealing wolves are waiting to tear him apart. He becomes the vicious amoral captor who Jonathan struggles to escape in the opening chapters. Descriptions of Dracula often draw on connotations of hell and evil. Jonathan notes Dracula's pleasure in seeing his distress, the

"...*red light of triumph in his eyes, and with a smile that Judas in hell might be proud of*".

Much of what the reader learns about Dracula in the rest of the narrative is pieced together in retrospect as Mina compares the journals, letters and newspaper sources over a number of months in England. Dracula has planned meticulously, travelling with boxes of Transylvanian earth to sleep in and landing at Whitby, where it would seem he has the power to shape-shift, becoming a dog or larger canine, transforming to a shadowy mist and a bat. This enables him to gain access to his victims and move through the tiniest of spaces. He also is able to manipulate the weather; this is seen in the appearance of fog as he sails. He transfers these abilities to Lucy when he attacks her.

Dracula's powers are somewhat limited in daylight hours, and he must keep the shape he has chosen from dawn to dusk. Jonathan notes that when seeing Dracula again in London that he appears much younger than he was on their first meeting. This highlights his powers of immortality. He would seem to draw life from the blood of his victims. They restore his strength and youth, although he still carries a scar from Jonathan's attack in Transylvania, much as Mina retains her scar until the curse is lifted. He requires native soil to sleep in during the day and this will prove to be a weakness when the men bless the soil and render most of his boxes useless to him.

Dracula's victims are seen to be predominantly female. While he cruelly mocks Mina in suggesting she has entered an unholy union in drinking his blood, his primary motivation is to gain power. When confronted by the young men in his Piccadilly home, he vows to corrupt "*your girls that you love*", but also asserts that he will eventually take and control the men.

Bram Stoker's Dracula: A Study Guide for A Level

In biting victims, he creates more vampires;

"For all that die from the preying of the Un-dead become themselves Un-dead, and prey on their kind. And so the circle goes on ever widening, like as the ripples from a stone thrown in the water."
(Chapter 16)

The group eventually take advantage of the fact that Dracula most often lies in a 'death sleep' during daylight hours to ambush the Count as he flees England. They use his telepathic powers against him, as his mental link with Mina enables her to be hypnotised and track some of his movements. In the final confrontation, Dracula himself is not staked but is stabbed in the heart by Quincey Morris while Jonathan Harker cuts at his throat in a form of decapitation.

Exploring the character of Jonathan Harker

A key protagonist in the narrative, Jonathan Harker is a solicitor who is sent from England to Transylvania to support Count Dracula in his purchase of Carfax Abbey in Purfleet, Essex. Harker has found the property and visits Dracula to finalise details. Harker is a typical example of the emerging Victorian middle class. He is keen on self-improvement, researching the area which he will visit. He demonstrates a degree of xenophobia and superiority in his complaints as he travels further East, reiterating colonial beliefs in differences between Western and Eastern Europe.

After a long and unsettling journey across Europe, including a late night coach journey through forests filled with wolves, he arrives at Castle Dracula. He is curious about his host, first finding him intelligent and proud, then finding to his horror that Dracula possesses supernatural characteristics, such as scaling down the wall like a lizard. Harker discovers that Dracula has menacing plans to travel around London creating more vampires. Harker is inquisitive, resembling an investigator in detective fiction.

Jonathan almost becomes a passive victim to three attractive female vampires in the castle. Dracula has imprisoned him and intends to dispose of him when his use has been served. Jonathan manages to overcome his fears and escapes the castle before collapsing of a brain fever at a convent. Mina is called to his sickbed, where they marry and although still weak from his encounters, Jonathan returns to England. Soon after, his employer and mentor dies, leaving him a house and legal firm.

In London to attend the funeral, Jonathan is horrified to see Dracula in the city. He joins Mina and Lucy's former suitors, who plan to pursue the Count. Harker's skills and experience as a lawyer enable him to investigate the Count's plans. He tracks down sources in Whitby and London.

Jonathan visibly ages as the narrative progresses, his hair turning white with exhaustion. He can still be resolute. He joins the others in neutralising Dracula's boxes of earth and chases the count from his Piccadilly home. He shares the group's belief about traditional gender roles. He agrees that Mina must be protected and not become involved in the physical pursuit. When Mina is found with Dracula Jonathan is guided by vengeance. He is willing to curse himself to Hell in order to save his wife from vampirism.

It is Jonathan who strikes the final blow - cutting Dracula's throat in what is effectively a decapitation. He also frames the narrative. His final note reaffirms the peace and stability provided by the model of family, celebrating his son Quincey and dismissing the file of records they have accumulated as just so much "typewriting". His attempts to dismiss their fantastical experiences perhaps do not do justice to Mina's careful compositions, and the novel's conclusion seeks to re-establish patriarchy. Mina quietly watches as Van Helsing praises her virtue in conversation with her son.

> **TASK: Jonathan Harker**
>
> What is your first impression of Jonathan Harker?
>
> On meeting the Count, what do his first actions and words reveal about his character?
>
> Remember to select relevant textual examples to support your views.

Women at work in a Victorian era office

Exploring the character of Mina Murray, later Mina Harker

Mina enters the novel as Mina Murray, close friend of Lucy Westenra and fiancée of Jonathan Harker. She works as a school mistress and is due to spend her summer holiday in Whitby with her close friend Lucy.

Mina is not a wealthy young woman but supports herself through work. She is similar to Jonathan in her commitment to self-improvement and expresses a desire to develop her shorthand and typewriting skills. She explains to Lucy this will help her support Jonathan in his legal work, but also has aspirations as a female journalist, committing to keeping a diary and writing regular letters to Lucy.

Mina has some of the characteristics of the much-maligned 'New Woman' in her independence and intellect, but is also seen to value traditional feminine roles, seeking to be a good and loyal wife to Jonathan and hoping to be a good mother in future. She provides Lucy with advice, and tries to protect her honour when she finds her sleepwalking in Whitby.

In place of traditional home-making tasks such as sewing and knitting, Mina stitches together the journals, letters, telegrams and news articles from various sources to build an empirical case for examination and establish a logical plan for fighting Dracula. She does fulfil the maternal role of comforter for the men in the group, supporting the grieving process for Lucy.

The reader may be surprised when Mina with her capable *"man's brain"* readily agrees to be ostracised from group discussions and left in the protection of the asylum when the men go to Carfax Abbey. She is frustrated but respects the decision, returning to her journal as a way of staying mentally active.

When she realises that Dracula has infected her, she is initially horrified at the contamination, labelling herself *"Unclean"*. She soon demonstrates courage and intellect in using her link with Dracula to discover his whereabouts.

Even in a weakened state, Mina tries to contribute and bravely asks the men to conduct funeral rites for her when she feels close to death. She may be suffering but she is able to have some pity for Dracula in his isolated and monstrous state.

Mina observes the men as they physically defeats Dracula and is then silenced in the text, the curse and scar lifted. Jonathan's postscript tells us that she has had a son, Quincey, and that the family have travelled to Transylvania and the castle as tourists.

Given the contradiction in the opening and closing notes framing the novel, it has been suggested that Mina may be the author of the introduction. She has been responsible for compiling records and ensuring all knowledge is shared. In putting records in chronological order she is the author of the narrative we are reading.

Exploring the character of Lucy Westenra

Lucy's letters to Mina reveal her as a joyful and kind young woman. Her beauty and kindness are noted by both Mina and the men who each wish to become her husband. She is courted by Arthur Holmwood, son of Lord Goldaming, Dr. John Seward, head of the Purfleet Asylum, and Quincey Morris, an American adventurer. Lucy jokes in a letter to Mina that she wishes she could marry all three. She is a dutiful daughter, choosing to marry Arthur, her mother's favourite and the one who can offer most financial security in the future. While Arthur is kind and a lifelong friend, she does hint that she is romantically attracted to Quincey and his cowboy tales.

Lucy's sense of freedom leaves her vulnerable to Dracula's attack. She sleepwalks to her fate and eventually dies, despite transfusions and nightly supervision. On her deathbed, her personality seems altered as she demands a passionate kiss from her fiancé Arthur. She snarls like an animal when she is refused.

The undead Lucy leaves her tomb and hunts for children, becoming known as the 'Bloofer', or beautiful, lady. As the men stand watch over her burial site, she tries to seduce Arthur once again, and undergoes a violent *"cleansing"* or second death, which releases her soul to Heaven.

Lucy is in one sense a scapegoat for uncontrolled female passions. Her sense of freedom and desire for romance, coupled with the lack of a male guardian, make her a culpable victim for Dracula. In dying, she has 'saved' Victorian womanhood from the threat of unchecked sexuality. Her death is also crucial to the narrative as it motivates her suitors to join forces with the Harkers and Van Helsing in their quest to stop Dracula.

Exploring the character of Dr John (Jack) Seward

Much of the narrative is presented to us through either Mina's journal or Seward's phonograph recording. His choice of audio recording equipment demonstrates a curiosity in technology which he shares with Mina, as well as being a sign of his professional role, as he uses the recordings to build a case study of his unusual asylum patient Renfield.

At the start of the narrative Seward attempts to deal with his disappointment at Lucy's rejection by turning to his work as director of the asylum at Purfleet. He is fascinated by Renfield's pursuit of immortality and records interviews and observations of him. Seward represents the rational and empirical mind of Victorian professionals. He applies the scientific method to all situations he encounters.

On hearing of Lucy's illness, he enlists the help of his old teacher and mentor, Doctor Van Helsing. He is initially puzzled by Van Helsing's use of garlic and religious items in Lucy's sick room and despite making scientific observations, cannot reconcile Lucy's deterioration with his medical knowledge.

He joins Van Helsing on a visit to Lucy's tomb despite his own scepticism, and while he cannot rationalise his experiences, he agrees to do everything in his power to free Lucy from vampirism and to combat Dracula.

Seward shows appreciation for Mina's intellect when he meets her and he is a key member of the group. He also controls what we learn of Van Helsing, often reporting the older doctor's lengthy explanations of Dracula's history and behaviours.

Jonathan notes in the concluding note that Seward has moved on from the experience and is now happily married.

Exploring the character of Arthur Holmwood, later Lord Goldaming

Holmwood is introduced in the narrative as the man who succeeds in gaining Lucy Westenra's acceptance of a marriage proposal. As the son of a lord, he represents the Victorian upper-class gentleman, with money from inheritance rather than industry.

Arthur is courteous and friendly with Lucy's rejected suitors Morris and Seward, whom he has known previously. Holmwood becomes Lord Goldaming on the death of his father. It is Arthur's capital and finance which provides critical support in the attempt to pursue Dracula across Europe.

Arthur is initially distraught and helpless as he watches his fiancée Lucy die, but is later able to undertake the cleansing ritual to save her souls and becomes an active participant in the hunt for Dracula. Arthur is a representative of the aristocracy and their values. He is on the side of right and offers his services for the common good.

Exploring the character of Quincey Morris

The young Texan man appears as one of Lucy's admirers. Like Dracula and Van Helsing, he is an outsider to English society. Lucy comments on and is charmed by his use of American slang, while Van Helsing notes his brave and courageous American blood will be the shape of things to come.

If Dracula is a symbol of the past and an Eastern threat to the British Empire, Quincey himself represents the emerging threat of America's future global dominance. While Stoker gives Morris many admirable qualities and shows him to be brave, sacrificing his life to stab Dracula in the heart, Quincey Morris is nevertheless tied to Dracula is some subtle ways. He is a character who has experience of vampire bats and vampirism, guessing Lucy's disease before Van Helsing shares the information. He also disappears into the night, at one point firing into the room to scare a bat. Some critics have gone as far as to suggest Quincey himself is a potential vampire.

Symbolically, he represents the new and emerging empire of the United States. Stoker may admire his robust nature and frank speech, but nevertheless Quincey does not survive the ordeal. The English men and women prevail. Quincey's contribution is acknowledged by Jonathan and Mina Harker, who name their son Quincey on his birth, a year after the deaths of Dracula and Quincey.

Exploring the character of Renfield

Renfield is described in a degree of objective detail as part of Doctor Seward's case study. A strong man of 59, with moments of both depression and mania, Renfield is a patient in the insane asylum under the supervision of John Seward. He has a process of catching and eating insects, spiders, birds and small animals in order of size, as a way of absorbing "life force", which he feels will provide immortality.

Renfield is linked to Dracula. His behaviour alters when he is near, while periods of calm are seen when Dracula is not at home in Carfax Abbey. The reader views Renfield through the psychologist's eyes. Renfield's story is not only a sub-plot, but an indication of the power of suggestion Dracula is capable of employing upon weak minds. There is eventual pity for Renfield, who dies horrifically having served his purpose of giving Dracula entry into the asylum.

Exploring the character of Van Helsing

While rarely given a chance to communicate directly with the readers, Van Helsing's colourful language style (idiolect) and unusual methods make him a memorable character.

Van Helsing is the distinguished and highly educated mentor of Dr John Seward. He holds qualifications in medicine and law, to name but a few. Dr Seward notes his many qualifications using *"etc.etc."*. Van Helsing travels to England from his base in the Netherlands to assist in the treatment of Lucy, and also oversees the confrontation of Dracula.

In a novel about vampirism, it is ironic that Seward had once saved Van Helsing by sucking out poison from a wound and preventing gangrene. The reader realises Van Helsing has diagnosed a vampire bite from his use of garlic and superstitious, and dares to use the new process of blood transfusions in an attempt to prolong Lucy's life.

Mina provides a description of Van Helsing in her first meeting. She notes his head seems "indicative of thought and power". It may be noted that descriptions of his "good-sized nose" and "big bushy brows" do recall elements of Dracula's description. There is a sense Van Helsing is Dracula's positive double. Both men are strong, intelligent outsiders, but they are perceived in very different ways.

Seward is keenly aware of Van Helsing's complex philosophical and scientific understanding. He also notes he has the "kindliest and truest heart that beats" when recommending him to Arthur Holmwood.

Van Helsing demonstrates the benefit of mature experience. When the three female vampires seek to tempt him outside the castle, he recognises their attractiveness as Jonathan had done, but can rationalise his own response and return to objectively destroying them.

Van Helsing does not directly attack Dracula at any point, although he provides the other men with the methods in which to do so. At the very close of the novel,

Quincey Harker sits on Van Helsing's knees as he visits Jonathan and Mina. Van Helsing praises Mina's virtue once again, as they look to the future.

Fathers are noticeable in their absence in the text. Lord Goldaming dies in the course of the narrative. Other fathers have already died or not mentioned. Jonathan's employer has been a mentor for him and dies leaving him a home and business. Van Helsing serves as a father figure to the group to some extent.

> **EXAM-STYLE RESPONSE: Men in the Novel**
>
> *In Dracula, Stoker challenges the nineteenth-century view of men as powerful.*
>
> With reference to Stoker's narrative methods, and relevant contextual information, show to what extent you agree with the above statement.

Minor Characters

Mrs Westenra

Lucy's mother is known for her weak heart and nerves, with the characters shielding her from the extent of Lucy's illness. She inadvertently thwarts Van Helsing's plans to protect Lucy by removing the garlic garlands and opening the windows, unwittingly giving Dracula access to her daughter. It is implied that she died of shock when encountering the vampire in Lucy's room.

Mr Swales

Mina singles out the retired fisherman in Whitby, using him as a source for local customs and legends. While he initially scoffs at tall tales and superstitions, he pays with his life on his encounter with Dracula and is found dead on the graveyard bench.

Swales is one of a number of working class characters presented by Stoker through the use of eye dialect. He uses non-standard English vocabulary and syntax to suggest both regional accent and local language variations. Stoker had spent time in Whitby compiling a glossary of local language variation.

Eyewitnesses

Throughout the text, in both newspaper clippings and journal entries, a number of men are interviewed about their encounters or dealings with Dracula. There are a range of accounts, from the zookeeper's report of a change in animal behaviour to superstitious sailors and drunken removal men.

These voices add a degree of authenticity and variety to the text, and serve to move the narrative forward. A number of the interviews are carried out by Jonathan Harker, and he is often keen to present generalisations about the working class, most often the need to bribe men to for information with the promise of an alcoholic drink, or "coin of the realm". These are prejudices shared by many in middle and upper class Victorian society and part of a larger fear of national degeneration. Britain had seen its overseas Empire decline, and following a series of economic recessions, there was a real fear that society was weak and morally bankrupt. Jonathan is often scathing about the men he encounters, and expresses no surprise that these corrupt and weaker characters could be involved with Dracula, an outside threat.

The Vampire Women

The three women who aim to seduce Jonathan in the castle are revealed as vampires who feed on local children. They are beautiful and horrifying in equal measure. They seem to have some emotional lives, as one expresses frustration that they have been cast aside by Dracula.

They are a vision of what Mina could become and call to her as a "sister" when they circle the campfire.

They represent the licentious version of womanhood most feared by the Victorians.

> **TASK: Minor Characters**
>
> *Consider the physical description of the vampire women.*
>
> *How does Stoker convey Harker's attraction to these women?*
>
> *How does Stoker convey Harker's fear and repulsion?*
>
> *How do their words and actions mark their 'monstrous sexuality'?*

Dracula's Men

Throughout the novel, small bands of men camp around the Castle and escort Dracula on his journey. They belong to ethnic groups originally subservient to Dracula and maintain their loyalty to him. Van Helsing's research and Dracula's own descriptions of his heritage would suggest they are a group of Roma origin. Harker refers to them as "gypsy" and as in his treatment of the workers in England, he suggests that their ethnicity aligns them to Dracula's immorality.

2.3 Themes and Symbolism

In this section we will;
- *Develop informed responses to Dracula, using associated concepts and terminology*
- *Analyse ways in which meanings are shaped in texts*
- *Explore literary texts informed by different interpretations*

Blood

Blood is used as a metaphor for race and sexual interaction throughout the text. It serves as both a substance and a cultural concept. It can signify passion and family ties, yet these same ties can also lead to violence and destruction in protecting blood kinships.

The text is reliant on blood imagery. Blood can simultaneously represent the thrill and excitement of life and passion, and the fear and terror of death. Both elements are united in the vampire. Dracula lives on the border between realms of the living and the dead. He feeds on blood, but he needs to nourish his living body. The biological function of blood is overtaken by human connection. Ultimately the extraction of blood becomes the extraction of the soul. Dracula lacks a soul and needs to feed to survive. Dracula subsists on souls. The women become his possessions. Vampirism is a racial threat against humans; it dehumanizes them. The text references immigration and cultural degradation. Blood was traditionally both the unity of family and the division of tribal conflict.

There is also a medical model linking sex and blood, based on prevailing knowledge. The exchange of blood had been regarded as a form of intercourse in the seventeenth and eighteenth centuries, building on a link being made between the exchange of fluids and the spread of disease. While medical models had begun to move beyond this belief, it is still evident in the text in the apprehensions surrounding the multiple transfusions that Lucy receives, and the fact that Arthur Holmwood believes the mixing of their blood to be a marriage in the sight of God. Lucy seems to revive on each transfusion and becomes lively, suggesting a pleasure which indicates her change into a vampire. Van Helsing also makes the link to promiscuity by joking that he has been unfaithful to his wife in sharing blood and deems Lucy a polyandrist for receiving blood from a number of men.

Dracula's 'otherness' is seen to trigger women's true and corrupt nature. Mina is already fiercely independent and strong and it can be argued that in conforming to conventions of feminine behaviour and submitting to the 'protection' of the asylum she is left open to Dracula's attack.

Sanity and rationality

Returning to the novel, nearly every character expresses doubt about their own sanity. Harker feels his journal helps him avoid insanity, although he eventually succumbs to a 'brain fever' having escaped the castle, Seward tries to rationalise what he has seen *"going in my mind from point to point as a model man, and not a sane one, follows an idea"* (Chapter 14).

Following Lucy's death Van Helsing frightens the others with his hysterical laugh, while Holmwood is said to be in hysterical grief over Lucy's fate. Renfield, although a minor character, becomes the "focal point of madness". These continued references to mental instability are an indication to the reader that there are *"no fixed borders between sanity and insanity"* (Pedlar, 2001).

Degeneracy

In the physical descriptions of Dracula, Harker and others rely upon making links between physical appearance and evaluation of morality and criminality. Darwin in his *Descent of Man* positioned men as superior to women and children in terms of evolution and intelligence, and in turn racial categorisation suggested certain men were more developed than others. These beliefs underpin many of Van Helsing's comments praising Mina's exceptional 'man's brain' and his confidence that as a group they can defeat Dracula, who possesses a 'child's brain'.

Further discussion will be presented on Lombroso and his work on criminality and Nordau's degeneracy theories, which proved popular with those in Victorian society who believed society was 'devolving' with the lower classes facing moral decline. While Dracula is an aristocrat he is known to marginal groups. It is also worth noting that while many Victorians did feel degeneracy was primarily affecting the lower classes, there were also fears relating to the practice of 'slumming', where upper and middle class men and women engaged in 'tourism' and illicit activities in the East End areas of London associated with crime.

Dangerous Sexuality

Voluptuous (OED) of a woman.

1. Attractive in a sexual way. Curvaceous and sexually attractive.

2. Relating to or characterised by luxury or sensual pleasure

from Late Middle English/ Old French.

In the 'cleansing ritual' the deceased Lucy is staked through the heart and decapitated in the hope that the process will save her mortal soul. The ritual is undertaken by men who use physical power and violence to drive out vampirism. Some critics have seen the staking as a symbolic rape and a violent reassertion of patriarchal power. Lucy is punished for her **'voluptuousness'**, a characteristic seen in her undead behaviour.

There are a number of instances when encounters with vampires are explicitly linked to sexuality and contagion. When Lucy and the female vampires are staked, the descriptions of "writhing forms" and animalistic breathing suggest a sensual or sexual element. Mina is horrified by her experience with Dracula. Having taken his blood in a subversion of a mother feeding a child, their blood is fused and she cries out that she is "Unclean!". As a male, Harker initially enjoys the sexual aggression of these women and confesses *"a wicked, burning desire that they would kiss me with those red lips"* but is ultimately submissive. There is a potential taboo in Dracula's intervention. He 'rescues' Jonathan by claiming *"This man belongs to me!"*

Stoker often expressed revulsion at overt references to sexuality in fiction and non-fiction texts. He condemned the acts of his compatriot and former acquaintance Oscar Wilde during his trials for indecency. Some critics do highlight that Stoker may have had enforced celibacy within his marriage following the birth of his first child to his wife Florence Balcombe. They suggest that there were rumours that Stoker caught syphilis from prostitutes in later life. These biographical details are seen as supporting a reading of the text as an expression of Stoker's own latent desires. We must take care with biographical readings such as these. Not only are they somewhat reliant on conjecture, but there was also a wider belief that a middle or upper class woman should only have sex in marriage to procreate rather than for personal pleasure and that is was not uncommon for some couples to lead essentially separate lives once children had been born.

Nearly New Women?

Victorian society expressed disquiet at the growing independence of women. The so-called 'New Woman' was described in terms of her likeness to a male in appearance and behaviour. A caricature of these women smoking and cycling ignored the aspirations to gain education, voting rights and access to vocation careers. The New Woman was seen as desiring to shock traditional sensibilities.

Mina demonstrates aspects of the feared 'New Woman' in her career, and her interest in learning and new technology. She has some control of her personal and professional life yet berates the New Woman for her liberal views on marriage. As a schoolmistress, Mina had experience as a leader and teacher. Her 'New Woman' tendencies are accepted as she uses her "man's brain" to help defeat Dracula.

Bram Stoker's Dracula: A Study Guide for A Level

Lucy resembles the 'New Woman' in her rebellious and flirtatious approach to relationships. Lucy may be considered to be over-familiar with her sexuality in a Victorian context, although her worst indiscretion is allowing a kiss from Quincey Morris after rejecting his proposal.

Mina survives as she combines tradition and modernity, much like Van Helsing. As a 'moderate' New Woman who eventually accepts her role as a wife and mother. Her commitment to Jonathan as a pure and loyal wife garners the complete support of the group.

Mina as 'Vampire' of Production and Consumption

Mina is an assistant schoolmistress, devoted wife and maternal shoulder to cry on. She presents herself as loyal and hard-working. Van Helsing deems her one of the *"good women still left to make life happy"*. He positions her in a traditional female role and is sure that she will *"make good lesson for the children that are to be"*.

However Mina is perhaps a sight for *"disputed femininity"*, sharing characteristics with the New Woman. She holds a passionate friendship with Lucy. Like the independent women who sought educational and professional fulfilment in medicine, nursing, education and the Typing Girl pools.

Hugh Stuffield in *Blackwood* magazine in 1895 was sharply critical of women with ideas:

"With her head full of all the 'ologies and 'isms, with sex-problems and heredity, and other gleanings from the surgery and the lecture-room, there is no space left for humour, and her novels are for the most part merely pamphlets, sermons, or treatises in disguise".

Others went further. Teachings on eugenics following Henry Manobley and Charles Harper suggested that overeducated women threaten well-being of the Empire. They argue that Nature will get its revenge on the 'muscular woman'. She will become a mother to the New Man. Men were not alone in these beliefs. Mrs Roy Devereux saw the rise of the New Woman as a reflection of the *"strange unloveliness"* of the world.

The New Women did respond. Sarah Grand was seen as the typical New Woman novelist and was highly critical of the behaviour of men in the patriarchal society, labelling them the "Bawling Brotherhood". She also levels criticism at those she labels the "cow-woman" and "scum-woman". The 'cow-woman' is the docile, unquestioning wife, while the 'scum-woman' is the woman carrying disease. Grand did not have pity for these women, and feels they share the blame with selfish men.

Grand also urged women to seek wider sexual knowledge as a way of preventing the spread of VD (venereal disease), particularly in situations were sexually transmitted diseases were spread to a wife following the husband's time with prostitutes. She did write the novel "The Heavenly Twins" to highlight how syphilis was spreading to married women from their husbands. This formed part of the wider public debate on the Contagious Diseases Act.

Writers such as George Egerton and Grant Allen presented the new woman as one who explored eroticism and was driven by a desire for sexual freedom. The Suffragists were against this type of woman and saw her as a threat to the status quo and an impediment to the fight for women's voting rights.

Harker constructs Mina as he imagines her while staying at the castle. His chivalric and romantic idealism are evident when he enters a room which he believes to have been the room where a fair lady has "*many blushes*" while writing an "*ill-spent love letter*". It is a fantasy of passive femininity, rudely disrupted by the appearance of the three women. He becomes the passive victim in a threat to conventional gender expectations. He is attracted to the women but immediately realises these responses would "*cause...pain*" to Mina. He maintains her as an ideal. He is repulsed by these female creatures; "*Faugh! Mina is a woman, and there is naught in common*". Their monstrous nature is placed in relief by her purity. Both Jonathan and later Van Helsing define Mina as a model of passive femininity. Lacking Mina's guidance Jonathan is uncertain and confused and although he manages to escape the castle, descends into a 'brain fever'.

For the reader, the interlacing narrative provided by Mina's letters challenge Jonathan's chivalric vision. Mina lists her numerous activities and projects, including developing shorthand and skills in typewriting. Mina keeps a journal to help Harker but also as a project in self-improvement. While this is a move away from the domestic sphere, some critics would argue her writing and gathering of information could be seen as a form of "*up-to-date housekeeping*".

The novel is a journalistic mix of text and voices, recrafted by Mina the journalist. Her commitment to work makes her an active agent. Writing enables Mina to develop a sense of self.

It is interesting to consider Mina's own criticism of the New Woman. She verges on embarrassment that their over-eating at tea in Robin Hood's Bay would shame a New Woman with a hearty appetite but then makes a series of reflections which are more ambiguous. She gazes on the sleeping Lucy and imagines herself in the place of Arthur. This contemplation of a male perspective is very much in line with the thinking of New Woman literature and while she seems dismissive of the possibility of the New Woman with her sexual freedom testing and proposing to a man, she does call it a "*consolation*", with the irony of the phrase "*nice job*" not wholly secure. Mina is perhaps more of a subversive thinker than she would dare to admit. This benefits the others as she creates the knowledge base which aids the destruction of Dracula.

There is one example of her persistent femininity and this is in her loyal vow to Jonathan not to read his journal from the time spent in the castle. Her ignorance is romanticised, as she seals the journal as a wedding gift. Mina claims complete trust but is genuinely relieved that he has not been with what Sarah Grand would have termed a 'scum-woman'. Mina claims she does not want to know but is pragmatic, opening and reading the journal when Jonathan seems troubled.

When typing the journal in triplicate Mina seems to torture herself with the details. Given that Jonathan's diary was in shorthand, it is possible that she has added the details to Jonathan's encounters, particularly the reference to the "*red lips*". She seems to be willing to share this publicly in order to protect others in future.

Mina's desire for knowledge seems to be a sign of her "*man's brain*". Soon afterwards she is ostracised from the band of men. Despite the fact that it is Mina who has composed the records, all the men agree that she "is better off out of it".

Some feminist critics have drawn attention to Mina's passionate friendship with Lucy. This is innocent but can be codified in the context of later Victorian society as a version of a "rave" or a "smash", a female crush on the part of the girlish Lucy, who is trying to impress the more sensible and mature Mina.

In the middle of the nineteenth century close female friendships were encouraged as a sign of true womanhood but in the age of the New Woman and debates on normality and deviance were viewed with suspicion. There was an ambiguity described by early psychologists such as Ellis who felt women with traces of masculinity were "inverted" and pathological. Studies were conducted, including large-scale interviews with girls who attended boarding schools and letters written in the 1860s and 70s were openly passionate, while those written later were a little more self-conscious in expressing feelings.

Lucy's writing style would seem to be that of the excessive school girl as she vows "*I love him!*" when discussing Arthur Holmwood in the conclusion of a letter detailing her day of proposals. Lucy does not seem wholly reliable as while this is an effusive declaration she also admits being attracted to Quincey. She does value Mina's friendship and idolises her much in the way that Jonathan presents Mina as being the ideal.

In her responses, the newly married Mina Harker presents herself as the role model of a dutiful wife. She looks forward to advising Lucy on her future role. Between the women there are moments when it is ambiguous as to whether they are speaking of each other of future partners. This excess of love and feeling is pure but can be exploited by the vampire. Given that the novel is in a Gothic rather than a realist mode the social and political can still be evidenced in her desire to work and deep friendship which suggest traits of the New Woman. As an outsider Dracula is a monster of prohibition - he attracts and repels in equal measure - and Mina's behaviours take her beyond the normal aspirations for motherhood. Passivity is imposed on her by the group of men, and Van Helsing's references to her future role as mother. Mina's differences give her a slim affinity with the Count. Mina herself can be seen as 'gothic' in her forming herself as a subject. She is cast out of the male adventure, joining Lucy and Dracula as a potential scapegoat. Just as social anxieties relating to Victorian sexuality are conflated in Dracula through his transgression and seduction, so too anxieties remain at the end of the text, when Mina is effectively silenced and put in her correct place as a mother.

Van Helsing highlights that knowledge is taboo for Mina in his repeated references to her "man's brain". As a doctor, scientist and psychiatrist Van Helsing not only evaluates Dracula but also reads the younger characters using concepts of degeneracy.

With the women, it is the extreme purity and femininity of Lucy and Mina that leave them vulnerable to destruction. Mina is perhaps more complex in that she has moments of affinity with Dracula. She can feel pity for his isolation and she is tied to him when both share a gaze towards a girl on a London street. Jonathan's end-note contains a silent Mina. Jonathan is glad she is a mother yet the opening note states all has been contained and there is a sense that Mina is author of all. In asking the reader to doubt, she has asked them to doubt Harker.

Dracula as a scapegoat?

Dracula was published two years after Max Nordau's *Degeneration* in 1895. Drawing on criminology of his mentor Lombroso, Nordau argued that modern life, be it trains, pollution, art or literature, was having a detrimental effect on middle-class society. It had been believed that working classes and outsiders were potentially criminal, but arguments now turned to the decadent writings of authors like Emile Zola and Oscar Wilde as evidence of degeneracy and weakness in the nation.

This tended to encourage scapegoating. If a moral crime can be seen as the responsibility of a socially marginalised person or group of people, purification can be achieved through exile or killing. The community will be cleansed. This can be seen in the treatment and fates of Lucy and Dracula, and to some extent in Mina, who loses her scar and embraces family life at the end of the story.

Dracula as monster is the perfect scapegoat. His plans and actions mark him as a monstrosity. The central irony is that the true monstrosity of Dracula is his similarity to those who chase him. He has financial means, he is intelligent, he has acquired enough English language and customs to blend in society. At the end of the narrative the community is cleansed by his death.

TASK: Examination Style Response

Dracula is a novel about the victory of good over evil.

With reference to Stoker's narrative methods, and relevant contextual information, show to what extent you agree with the above statement.

You can consider Dracula as scapegoat within this response.

2.4 Setting – Crossing Boundaries

In this section we will;
- *Develop informed responses to Dracula, using associated concepts and terminology*
- *Analyse ways in which meanings are shaped in texts*
- *Explore literary texts informed by different interpretations*

Whole Text Analysis: Settings

Analysis of settings requires the reader to consider the places described and how these may relate to the themes of the novel. A key movement in the novel is the relocation to France in the final chapters.

There is an implied relationship between geography and morality. Crossing the English Channel and travelling East provides a metaphor for crossing social and moral boundaries. The physical changes in landscape reflect psychological changes and moral freedom.

Dracula as Travel Narrative

Gothic texts often drew on the travel narrative. While early Gothic used the journey as a metaphor for psychological development, Stoker used the genre to present ideological themes.

Harker adopts a typical Orientalist perspective. The reference to shorthand would be familiar to readers as a device to suggest immediacy and objectivity. He complains about the disruption to train services as he travels further East. He employs the generic convention of the crossing of the river symbolising a move from civilisation to the wilderness. This is a subtle critique of colonial superiority, as Harker regards everything as a diverting spectacle. There is a degree of mirroring in Dracula's and Jonathan's characters; Dracula studies Bradshaw's railway guides while Harker loves trains. Dracula studies English history and geography while Harker researched travel guides in the British Library.

Dracula undermines any sense of stable opposition as in some ways he is the most 'Western' character. He uses his knowledge to exploit a country and its people, proving an uncomfortable reflection of British imperial practice.

The Victorian reader cannot place him clearly as *'Other'*. They are unsettled by the fact he can borrow Jonathan's suit and pass as him in the local village. Later, he will be able to mingle in London. In Kipling's text, characters go undercover for law and order, while Dracula does this to disrupt order. Stoker never explicitly acknowledges continuity between Dracula and British imperial practices.

Van Helsing uses a metaphor of degeneracy suggesting that Dracula is a child struggling to manhood. He fails to recognise that Dracula is immortal and will have infinite time to develop his plan. This is where the real threat lies- it predicts the fall of the British Empire.

It is interesting that the novel 'ends' twice. Dracula's death is overshadowed by Jonathan's note. Dracula is extinguished by a kukri knife and a bowie knife, weapons of empire. It is noteworthy that Quincey also dies, extinguishing America's growing threat to Britain.

Morris has been linked with the vampire and other outsiders. Lucy compares his tales to Othello regaling Desdemona. Morris is also the character who makes an explicit reference to vampires in response to Lucy's illness. Morris and America provide a threat as the growing strength may supplant Britain.

England's final triumph over Dracula is qualified. Quincey Harker has made the Harkers a family. Dracula's blood has formed part of the future race. The baby is born on the anniversary of the death of Dracula and Quincey. The child can be seen to have Dracula's blood and Quincey's spirit. The child is the future but also a reminder of the violent past. The final references made to the holiday in Transylvania recalls the travel narrative and Gothic style of the opening journal entries. The text has come full cycle. Harker firmly regards the papers gathered as mere typewriting. In asserting the lack of substance he creates a reverse effect. The attempt to erase is not just physical but psychological. In refusing the text, Harker undermines his wife's work and the opening note.

Englishness, the East and morality

Critical readings are often concerned with the relationship between the representation of the physical world and the potential ideologies such representations would seem to support. While less concerned with the dichotomy between the 'old' and 'new' worlds of England and America - although these are referenced in the characterisation of Quincey Morris – Stoker presents a focus on a narrow section of predominantly middle-class London society and contrasts this with the apparent threats presented as coming from Eastern Europe and beyond.

The 'East' is symbolic of terror throughout the novel. Harker describes Eastern Europe as an area of unknown beliefs and practices. His arrival on the East Yorkshire coast in Whitby brings death and horror to the town. He purchases Carfax, thought to be Purfleet, on the East side of the Thames, with further properties bought in Whitechapel and Bermondsey. The symbolism not only relies on Orientalist models of the East as opposition to the rational 'civilised' London, but also a conflation of East and the East End. The female vampires have a visible sexuality and aggression which recalls the prostitutes known in Whitechapel.

Dracula's ability to move undetected through London's crowded streets tapped into the contemporary fears about uncontrolled immigration. Ghetto communities were seen as contributing to increased levels of crime in London. Dracula's lairs suggest he moves in this underworld, with Chicksand Street being in Whitechapel, made notorious by the 'Jack the Ripper' killings in 1888, and Bermondsey being the home of Jacob's Island the 'rookery' of crime made famous in *Oliver Twist*.

The 'Ripper' murders not only created press hysteria, but also lead to victimisation of the local Jewish community, as it was felt that someone from the Jewish ghetto had committed the crime and was being protected by others. The fears of immigrants such as Dracula fuelled the introduction of *The Aliens Act of 1905*, which was largely implemented to control immigration from Eastern Europe.

TASK: 'Englishness' and Morality

It is worth reflecting on the following:

- How does the world beyond England's boundaries feature in the narrative?

- How is the relationship between 'English' and 'foreign' elements conceptualised and explored?

- What values, qualities or possibilities are implicit or explicit here?

2.5 The 'Other'

In this section we will;
- *Develop informed responses to Dracula, using associated concepts and terminology*
- *Analyse ways in which meanings are shaped in texts*
- *Explore literary texts informed by different interpretations*

Dracula, monstrous trespasser

The monster is the Gothic presentation of 'the *Other*'.

Society can create monsters through 'othering'. At its root, monstrosity is based on difference and a failure to conform. Traditional myths created monsters based on what humanity was not. Monsters were identified by animalistic features. By the nineteenth century the monster was a product of society, in opposition to rational behaviour and thought. A prime example is seen in The Strange Case of Dr Jekyll and Mr Hyde. Imperial Gothic monsters are liminal 'others', inhuman yet familiar.

There was a humanization of the supernatural, as the monster was given traits and motivations. These monsters served as embodiments of fears of modernized world, often linked to developments in science and colonialism. The Gothic monster saw elements of the rational civilised world combine with irrational, chaotic human fantasy.

The monster is also a product of humanity as they are 'birthed ' by humans, developed in the author's imagination. When Stoker was writing, England was seen as the 'civilised centre'. The decline of political and economic power created anxiety. The 1890s threatened a ghostly return to the past. Dracula was published as the Empire was in decline. There was a real fear of regressing into a primitive state.

Dracula is a monstrous trespasser. He materialises difference. As an immigrant he fosters a fear of the unknown. The text could be seen as the presentation of atonement. Dracula enacts reverse colonialism and so may be regarded as a deserved punishment for the violence enacted on other nations.

The link to the colonial mind-set is evident in Harker's opening journal entries, which bears the characteristics of the 'travel narrative'. Throughout the description of the journey reference is made to boundaries. Throughout the narrative characters are seen maintaining and transgressing boundaries. England will have to be held accountable. Vampirism is a monstrous illness and will provide retribution for the corruption of imperial capitalism.

Dracula makes the monstrous familiar. He has raw economic power, and has acquired language and culture. However the rules make him an outsider, representing a past forgotten in Victorian world. He is unable to join modern society and is rejected by the English who fear he may bring the downfall of Western civilisation, through his creation of "semi-demons".

Monster OED

A large, ugly and frightening imaginary creature. When applied to humans, "an inhumanity cruel or wicked person".

Liminality

Characteristics relating to being in transition, or occupying a position on, or at both sides of, a boundary or significant threshold. Dracula is in transit from East to West and occupies a space between the human

Bram Stoker's Dracula: A Study Guide for A Level

Dracula is a product of Gothic heritage. He presents a history full of tribal migrations and conquests. He has pride in his militaristic, warrior past. Dracula values blood and honour.

This seems to be the binary opposition of Victorian values. Dracula is transgressive as he does not answer to human ethics. He seems irrational and therefore threatens stability.

Dracula's vampirism also creates an infection of the soul. In contemporary non-fiction, vampirism had been linked to syphilis. This was a common simile for disease. His infection degrades humans and dehumanised them. Vampirism provides the antithesis of humanity. The group must eradicate the danger he presents to restore order and balance.

Dracula is not the only outsider in the text. At various points the 'foreign' nature of Van Helsing, Quincey Morris and Renfield are noted. It is worth also noting that these characters remain recorded voices in the text, mediated through the controlling figures of Mina or Seward. Lucy and Harker also contribute, creating a *"middle class hegemony"* (Halberstrom, 2003) in the presentation of the narrative.

The writing is controlled and becomes an indication of knowledge and power. Likewise, Mina's reading is curtailed when she is under Dracula's power, as she is now seen as having the power to be corrupt and dangerous if she unconsciously gives Dracula access to their information.

Dracula has no voice - *"he is read and written by the other characters in the novel"* (Halberstrom, 2003). It can be argued that his silence increases his power.

This can be seen as a mechanical text as it is explicitly concerned with the technologies of production - typewriters, phonographs, telegrams, and shorthand, among others.

Van Helsing bears an interesting relationship to the other characters. The Netherlands is situated between England and Transylvania and likewise Van Helsing seems familiar with both worlds. He produces a solution as he is aware of both the rational and supernatural. He is a source of essential knowledge yet is not directly involved in the murder.

There are negative elements to Van Helsing's character. He harbours both gender and class prejudices. For him, the female's only role is procreation. In recognising the affinities between Dracula and Van Helsing it can be argued women are equally subjugated. Dracula could be read as a parody of sanctioned exploitation practised by Western males. The most horrific is when the 'Other' becomes familiar. Given that Stoker was Irish; a post-colonial reading highlights the brutality of British rule in Ireland and violence such as the 1882 Phoenix Park murders showing the consequences of imperial domination.

Victorians may have recognised models of imperial ideology, reflected back through a gothic mirror. Before Dracula invades bodies or lands, he invades bodies. He can survive in various roles. Dracula presents an ironic reflection, an Occidental scholar studying all things Western while Harker dismisses Oriental or Eastern societies; a warrior nobleman in contrast to the dying Lord Goldaming. He is both a mimic and a reversal of traditional expectations.

Women were expected to be models of domesticity. In the novel women are seen as representative of corruptible purity. As future life bringers, they hold society's future. Both Lucy and Mina sense Dracula's arrival.

When Lucy is victimised, she loses her identity. Her life fades and her soul is consumed. When un-dead, Lucy targets the future in abducting and harming children. This is another example of reverse colonisation, as women actively target future generations.

Vampirism is a systematic intelligent disease. It avoids resilient populations such as the young and capable men. It exploits the vulnerable.

TASK: Fear of Disease

Consider the ways in which Stoker creates **a sense of fear** in *Dracula*.

You must relate your discussion to relevant contextual factors.

You should explore how fears are presented.

> A writer who attempts in the nineteenth century to rehabilitate the ancient legends of the were-wolf and the vampire has set himself a formidable task. Most of the delightful old superstitions of the past have an unhappy way of appearing limp and sickly in the glare of a later day, and in such a story as *Dracula*, by Bram Stoker (Archibald Constable and Co., 8vo, pp. 390, 6s.), the reader must reluctantly acknowledge that the region for horrors has shifted its ground. Man is no longer in dread of the monstrous and the unnatural, and although Mr. Stoker has tackled his gruesome subject with enthusiasm, the effect is more often grotesque than terrible. The Transylvanian site of Castle Dracula is skilfully chosen, and the picturesque region is well described. Count Dracula himself has been in his day a medieval noble, who, by reason of his "vampire" qualities, is unable to die properly, but from century to century resuscitates his life of the "Un-Dead," as the author terms it, by nightly draughts of blood from the throats of living victims, with the appalling consequence that those once so bitten must become vampires in their turn. The plot is too complicated for reproduction, but it says no little for the author's powers that in spite of its absurdities the reader can follow the story with interest to the end. It is, however, an artistic mistake to fill a whole volume with horrors. A touch of the mysterious, the terrible, or the supernatural is infinitely more effective and credible.

Part Three: Textual Commentary and Analysis

Part Three:
Textual Commentary and Analysis

3.1 *"Our ways are not your ways"*: Chapters 1-4
3.2 *" Tell me all the news when you write...."*: Chapters 5-7
3.3 *"So far there is much that is strange"*: Chapters 8-16
3.4 *"Your girls that you all love are mine already"*: Chapters 17-23
3.5 *"We shall follow him, and we shall not flinch..."*: Chapters 24-27

3.1 "*Our Ways are Not Your Ways*": Chapters 1-4

In this section we will;

- Consider how language and imagery convey writer's intentions in Dracula
- Evaluate the methods employed by Stoker to convey the patterns of natural speech and thought processes
- To show understanding of how Stoker's choice of form, structure and language shapes meanings.

Introduction

The text is subtitled "*A Mystery Story*". Stoker was influenced by earlier popular detective fictions such as Wilkie Collins's *The Woman In White*. Dracula shares the epistolary style and the questionable reliability of the narrators with the earlier text, as well as the framing device of the introductory note.

Preface/ Opening Note

This brief note claims that there follows a sequence of papers. The author of the note indicates that the narrative has been shaped and edited. It is an authoritative voice which explains "*all needless matters have been eliminated*". The preface recognises that the story that follows may defy belief. It confirms that all that follows will be "*simple fact*". It does make a claim for veracity and truth, stating that "*no statements of past things wherein memory may err*" are presented. It also notes that the records are "*exactly contemporary*".

Despite the central conflict between human and supernatural forces, and the use of the ancient threat of the vampire, the narrative foregrounds and celebrates modernity. Throughout, superstition is contrasted with rational and realistic detail. The Preface prepares the reader for the fantastic as it recognises " *a history almost at variance with the possibilities of latter-day belief*", before asserting that all will be presented as rational and "*simple fact*".

Chapter 1

The material presented is noted as being from Jonathan Harker's journal, originally inscribed in shorthand. Harker is seen to be a precise record keeper. There is some reference to his domestic relationships as he jots a reminder to ask for a recipe for Mina. These early entries read like an enthused travelogue.

Epistolary novels rely on subjective points of view, providing a precursor to the modern psychological novel. Jonathan's shorthand journal provides a detailed account of sociological and historical information relating to the country he is visiting.

Bram Stoker's Dracula: A Study Guide for A Level

Harker has a degree of confidence as he tries to make use of his "*smattering of German*". This invokes the Victorian model of 'self-help' or auto-didactism when Jonathan recounts the research he carried out on Transylvania to support him in dealing with his client, "*a nobleman of that country*".

	Shorthand
	Shorthand was developed to aid efficiency and productivity in the transcription of legal and journalistic documents.

Liminality

Characteristics relating to being in transition, or occupying a position on, or at both sides of, a boundary or significant threshold. Dracula is in transit from East to West and occupies a space between the human and supernatural.

The location Harker is travelling to is "*in the extreme East*", signifying its opposition to the perceived stability of London and western capitalism. It is on the border of three states and as such could be seen as in a liminal state. Likewise, it is in the midst of the mountains, presented as the "*wildest*" and "*least known*" area. Harker cannot locate the castle on a map, suggesting an exploration in to the unknown.

There is an implied domesticity as Harker provides motivation for his style of note-making, as a way of refreshing his memory when he tells Mina of his trip. There is a focus on providing dates and times, perhaps reflecting Jonathan's professional role as a solicitor's clerk.

He notes that Transylvania has multiple nationalities, with the groups listed being traced back over centuries. He notes the Szekelys, inhabitants of Count Dracula's region, claim links with Attila the Hun. In places, Harker's style imitates an encyclopaedia entry.

Harker establishes himself as an 'Orientalist', seeing a clear division in the behaviour and customs of those in Western and Eastern Europe. There is an initial suggestion of barbarism and violence, coupled with superstition. He decides that the region he is travelling to is wild, as he cannot chart it on a British map of Europe.

There is a tone of superiority but also curiosity as Harker plans to ask the Count about the beliefs and folklore of the "*imaginative whirlpool*". The image here foreshadows the danger he will later face.

ATHENA CRITICAL GUIDES

Stoker then presents the typical Gothic trope of a protagonist failing to sleep due to nightmares. This is immediately debunked by Harker's rational personality, as he explains his dreams a being the result of a dog howling nearby and having had spicy paprika before bed.

The constant focus on trains and timetables underlines the wider contrast between the rational and the fantastic. Jonathan is a logical character who approves of routine. Again this is framed in an opposition of East and West, as he relates lateness with Eastern territories. The language reflects this as the train is said to *"dawdle through"* the country.

There are highly descriptive passages which acknowledge the natural beauty of the county. He is less enamoured with the people and seems rude when he observes;

"The women looked pretty, except when you got near them..."

Harker imposes his imperial attitude on the Slovak people, marking them as *"more barbarian"* than others. He compares them to stage villains and links to ideas of 'Oriental'.

Orientalism

Refers to the study of near and far Eastern cultures, languages and societies. It can also refer to the representation of Eastern cultures in Western literature, design and art.

In the opening chapters, Harker takes an Orientalist perspective in his observations of Eastern European people and customs. He is influenced by the prejudices of imperialism and deems his own views and behaviours superior to those encountered. He uses the term 'barbarian' to describe the Slovak men, criticises the slow-running trains and comments on the superstitions and use of Catholic religious objects to ward off evil.

Crossing Boundaries

> **Transylvania**
>
> Transylvania translates as land 'beyond the forest'.

Chronology and calendar are important in the text. Times of day are symbolic throughout the text. There is a sense of dramatic irony, as readers aware of characters of Gothic and supernatural fiction may note the significance of Harker arriving at Bistritz *"on the dark side of twilight"*.

Again the age and position of the frontier or border is noted. Transylvania itself roughly translates as *"across or beyond the forest"*. There is a sense that Harker is at the threshold of human and supernatural, moving from the known to the unknown. Bistritz itself has a history of violence, suffering from fires, siege, famine and disease.

The Garden Krone hotel is also *"old-fashioned"* and Harker is pleased to meet a *"cheery"* owner who smiles and welcomes him.

Dracula is first introduced to the narrative through a letter which he has left for Harker at the hotel. It gives details of the onward journey in a small carriage or diligence, with a wish that Harker *"Sleep well tonight"*. Harker is puzzled by the change in behaviour of the hotel owners. The landlord acts as though he cannot understand German, while his wife looks at Jonathan in a *"frightened"* way. The couple cross themselves, making the sign of a cross used in Christian prayer. The old woman returns to Harker's room in hysterics, urging him not to travel further.

The hotel landlady explains that the 4th May is St. George's Eve and stresses the fear that at midnight

> *"all the evil things of the world would have full sway"*.

Harker has recorded the speech of those he encounters and this will become a feature of the journal entries, as the voices of many characters are mediated through diaries and recordings.

Harker notes the landlady's behaviour and his own reactions. There is an assertion of the rational when he describes her fear as *"very ridiculous"* but also shows honesty when he notes he *"did not feel comfortable"*. He is bound to his business and his duty, which he sees as *"imperative"*.

While Harker's belief in the Anglican faith means he sees the use of a Catholic crucifix as *"idolatrous"*, he takes the cross from her, claiming the action as good manners. He does admit in his journal that he keeps the crucifix on and that he is *"uneasy"*. In a startling break from the rational he records *"If this book should ever reach Mina before I do, let it bring my good bye. Here comes the Coach!"*

The journal entries for the 3rd and 4th May establish Harker as a rational and logical man. He presents his journal as a travelogue, noting the food, local dress, geography and history of Transylvania. He adopts a superior tone in his complaints about the lack of punctuality of trains.

Stoker will present a series of voices or narrators in the text and even in the early stages highlights that they may be unreliable. Harker seems to be trying to convince himself that the superstitions are nonsense when claiming to accept the landlady's crucifix to avoid offending her, yet a short time later asking that his journal be a final testament and goodbye to his love, Mina.

In the entry for the 5th May, there is a noticeable shift in language and vocabulary. The horizon seems *"jagged"* and Harker has *"odd things"* to note in his journal. He begins in a similar style of travel writing to the opening, noting his dinner of *"robber steak"* and the wine, stressing that he only had two glasses.

There seems to be conversations about him as the coach departs and Harker struggles to translate the various languages, but claims to pick up disturbing words such as *"Satan"*, *"hell"*, *"werewolf"* and *"vampire"*. The blessings and use of sign to ward off the 'Evil Eye', along with the pity all seems to direct towards Harker deepen the mystery.

The 'Evil Eye'

The 'Evil Eye' is believed to be a curse from the devil, given through an ill-meaning stare.

A number of European cultures believe it to result in injury or misfortune. The curse of evil can be defended against with certain gestures, the most used being the 'horned hand', the index finger and little finger to create horns on a clenched palm.

Objects in the shape of a blue eye are also called 'Evil Eyes' and are believed to protect against evil.

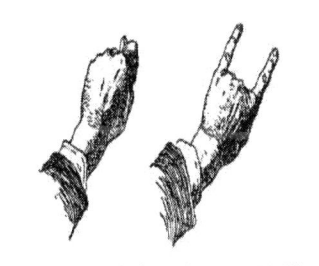

Två fingertecken (*la fica, le corna*), som i Italien brukas till skydd mot "onda ögon".

Once alone, Jonathan dismisses "*ghostly fears*" and resumes his style of travel writing. Initially it is a pastoral scene, green and full of fruit blossom. There are some discordant notes, as the pine woods are compared to "*tongues of flame*" and the road is "*rugged*".

Transylvania

Transylvania translates as land 'beyond the forest'.

The afternoon sun brings beauty to the scene, particularly as it shines on the snow-capped peal named "*God's seat*". As the sun sets the shadows "*creep*" and Harker notes crosses and shrines along the roadside. As evening approaches it becomes cold and "*the growing twilight seemed to merge into one dark mistiness the gloom of the trees*". Twilight and mist are typical features of the Gothic genre as both again suggest liminal states.

TASK: Crossing Boundaries

To what extent does Stoker suggest that Harker has journeyed to a world beyond Victorian society?

A sense of threat

Danger and threat now surrounds them, the driver refusing to let Harker get out and walk as the area fills with '*fierce dogs*'. Darkness seems to frighten the other travellers as the speed makes the vehicle sway "*like a boat tossed on a stormy sea*".

The passengers insist on giving Harker gifts along with blessings against the evil eye. The weather is stormy and threatening thunder. The unusual interaction between the coach driver and the carriage suggests there was a plea to be early and take Harker on to Bukovina.

The carriage driver is described by his

"*bright eyes, which seemed red*", his "*hard-looking mouth with very red lips and sharp-looking teeth, as white as ivory*".

A passenger quotes a known poem "*For the dead travel fast*".

The final let of the journey is noted for its speed and Harker's confusion and concern that they seemed to be travelling in circles. The mystery is heightened as Harker notes it is close to midnight "*with a sick feeling of suspense*". This is not improved when dogs begin to howl in every direction. Blue flames appear and the driver dismounts to mark their locations. Harker believes he is dreaming as this repeated a number of times.

They are surrounded by wolves, which add to the sense of the uncanny, as the driver would seem to have control over them and nature. The wolves move away following his "*imperious command*". Harker cannot rationalise through his own experience - he finds it all "*strange and uncanny*". The novel plays on the contrasting symbolism of light and dark, as the "rolling clouds obscured the moon".

The setting of; "*a vast ruined castle, from whose tall black windows came no ray of light, and whose broken battlements showed a jagged line against the sky*" serves to emphasis the sense of darkness and decay.

Bran Castle

Chapter 2

The journal entry for the day continues into Chapter 2. The series of updates add to the sense of there being a mystery to solve. Journals are used as a form of reflection throughout the novel. Eventually, record-keeping will form the basis of a strategic plan to defeat evil in the text.

The text reportedly refers to states of sleeping and waking. Harker emphasises how intimidating and imposing the courtyard seems. The strength of the driver is noted as "*prodigious strength*" with a crushing grip "*like a steel vice*". The door has "*large*" nails in a doorway of "*massive*" stone.

Gaps and silences are presented. Harker is unsure of how to gain entry as "*Of bell or knocker there was no sign*". Harker asks himself a series of questions about the "*grim adventure*" he has embarked upon. He notes his recent promotion to "*full-blown solicitor*" from clerk. His uncertainty is described as "*a horrible nightmare*". He is awake and alone.

Crossing the threshold

The reader has been given a description of Dracula. Harker sees a *"tall old man"*. He is dressed wholly in black and invites him in *"with a courtly gesture"*. He seems a mannered host as he speaks;

"Welcome to my house! Enter freely and of your own free will!"

This introduces the liminal motif which recurs throughout the novel. In entering the castle, Harker moves from the realm of the living and the dead. He has crossed this threshold himself.

Harker finds Dracula imposing, surprised by the strong handshake which is *"cold as ice, more like the hand of a dead than a living man"*. Harker guides the reader to the site of horror and mystery.

There is a strange juxtaposition between the Count's *"courtly"* bow and the fact that he carries Harker's luggage. This is explained by the lateness of Harker's arrival - Dracula claims his servants have gone home for the evening.

They pass through numerous doors, increasing the sense of mystery, although Harker is somewhat cheered by the welcoming log fire and *"the light and warmth and the Count's courteous welcome"*.

Stoker makes use of multiple texts and has Dracula reading aloud to Harker the letter sent by his employer Mr. Hawkins. This gives the reader the opportunity of learning more about Jonathan Harker, who is described by Hawkins as *"full of energy and talent"*, with *"a very faithful disposition"*. He is praised for his ability to be *"discreet and silent"*.

The Count seems interested in Harker and asks him questions, while Jonathan takes the opportunity to study his new client:

> *His face was a strong, a very strong, aquiline, with high bridge of the thin nose and peculiarly arched nostrils, with lofty domed forehead, and hair growing scantily round the temples but profusely elsewhere. His eyebrows were very massive, almost meeting over the nose, and with bushy hair that seemed to curl in its own profusion.*
>
> *The mouth, so far as I could see it under the heavy moustache, was fixed and rather cruel-looking, with peculiarly sharp white teeth.*
>
> *These protruded over the lips, whose remarkable ruddiness showed astonishing vitality in a man of his years. For the rest, his ears were pale, and at the tops extremely pointed. The chin was broad and strong, and the cheeks firm though thin. The general effect was one of extraordinary pallor. Hitherto I had noticed the backs of his hands as they lay on his knees in the firelight, and they had seemed rather white and fine. But seeing them now close to me, I could not but notice that they were rather coarse, broad, with squat fingers. Strange to say, there were hairs in the centre of the palm. The nails were long and fine, and cut to a sharp point. As the Count leaned over me and his hands touched me, I could not repress a shudder. It may have been that his breath was rank, but a horrible feeling of nausea came over me, which, do what I would, I could not conceal.*

Physiognomy

The study of how facial features or body types may link to psychological characteristics. It has ancient roots and was later revisited by Cesare Lombroso (1835-1909) who used it in criminal anthropology to suggest there were criminal types.

Harker is referencing physiognomy in his description of Dracula.

Harker has been engaging in a discredited 'science' from earlier in the nineteenth century related to physiognomy. The "*massive eyebrows*" would have been noted by the Victorian reader, who was familiar with Lombroso's work on appearance and criminality. These studies were not treated wholly seriously in Stoker's time - later in the novel he has Van Helsing gently mock Harker's evaluation of appearance - but the marker of the bushy eyebrows which meet in the middle would have been seen as an indicator of criminal tendencies or a dark psychology.

Likewise, the reference to the hairy palms seems bestial and suggest a devolved human. The implication of potential brutishness is reinforced by the description of his "*cruel-looking mouth*". Readers familiar with gothic horror will be more aware than Harker that the "*peculiarly sharp white teeth*" are a sign of the vampire. The "*ruddy*" lips seem an unusual feature to comment on in a man, and the juxtaposition of red on white will become a key signifier in the tale. Finally, Harker's nausea at the rank breath confirms the threat, although it is an indicator of the potential unreliability of the narrator when he notes this 'may' have been what made him nauseous.

Bram Stoker's Dracula: A Study Guide for A Level

The Count unsettles Jonathan further when he praises the howling wolves as "*children of the night*". He is somewhat scathing of Jonathan as a city dweller and feels he will always lack sympathy with the hunter. The horror of what Dracula hunts has not yet been revealed. Jonathan seems overwhelmed by the "*sea of wonders*" he has experienced. The water imagery recalls the reference to local superstitions as a whirlpool and is used throughout as a metaphor for lack of control. Harker tries to rationalise his emotions and fears he thinks "*strange things*". He notes that he has talked with the Count until dawn, and so is invited to sleep later the following day. Jonathan notes the Count's unusual routines. Dracula has a peculiar perspective, remarking "*how few days go to make up a century*".

The usually punctilious Harker misses the 6th May and on his entry for the 7th May notes the rest and enjoyments of the previous day. As in the opening pages, he returns to the perspective of the outside observer. He finds the disparity between the luxurious god dishes and fabrics, and the apparent lack of servants in a castle of such size. He is pleased to discover that the Count's library is packed full of English books and newspapers. This links the two men, as the Count seems as fond of research and preparation for his move to London as Jonathan has been on his travels.

Mastery

Dracula expresses his desire to live in London and assimilate with London society, "*to share its life, its change, its death*". He continues by expressing his desire to learn correct intonation and pronunciation of English from Jonathan. While he seems to have a very proficient grasp of the language he does not wish to be taken advantage of by others who realise he is an immigrant. This is also linked to his need for control and power:

"*I have been so long master that I would be master still*".

Harker is given free range of the castle, barring the locked rooms. Dracula warns Harker that "*our ways are not your ways, and there shall be to you many strange things*". The echoing of Jonathan's 'strange thoughts' increases the sense of uncanny and disruption of the familiar. Much of the evening's conversation is glossed, but Harker does record Dracula's explanation of the superstition and lore surrounding the mysterious blue flames. It involved recognition of the turbulent history of the region, where "*hardly a foot of soil in all this region has not been enriched by the blood of men*". This blood is conflated with the spoils of war. On St George's Eve, the treasure is said to be at the site of the blue flames but locals are too scared to look, as this also indicates a spirit. Dracula refers to his need for native soil; this will become evident in the transportation of boxes of earth to England later in the narrative.

Dracula makes a brief linguistic slip of the sort he is trying to avoid when he calls Jonathan "*Harker Jonathan*" using the name order familiar in his own language. Harker then recounts how he located the perfect property to match Dracula's brief. It seems strange that he seeks a house which is ancient and in disrepair. There is a digression as Jonathan notes Carfax derives from 'Quatre Face', indicating a crossroads. This location has supernatural connotations, as it is deemed a point where humans can barter their souls with the devil.

It sounds equally unappealing when Jonathan informs his that the property is in an isolated location, the only neighbour an asylum. Harker notes that he did not have the key for part of the property. In the text, keys often become synonymous with knowledge and power. Harker's lack of keys often places him in peril. The reader is reminded that this is still a modern text when he produces the Kodak pictures to show Dracula his new home. Photography was a relatively recent technology and allowed information to be conveyed across distances.

Dracula explains his preference for an ancient property by stating that he is from an old and noble family. He is relieved that the house has a private chapel which is not a home for the "*common dead*". There is a sense of negation in his list of what he does not look for - he is not interested in happiness, sunshine and sparkling water. He claims he has had "*weary years of mourning*", leading him to prefer shade and shadow. Harker is confused, as Dracula seems to say this with a smile. It is also noted that Dracula has marked London, Exeter and Whitby on his map. Once again, the men talk for many hours after supper. The coming dawn is li the "*turn of the tide*", which has links to belief about death.

Carfax, a liminal space

Crossroads are believed to be liminal spaces, which allow a crossing to other worlds. They present a point where a traveler must choose their future. Many European cultures traditionally buried suicides at crossroads, with the implication that these people were beyond the grace of Heaven. Dracula's main residence in London is named Carfax (an anglicisation of 'Quatre Face'), which suggests it is located at space between Heaven and Hell. The next-door asylum houses those at the boundary between sanity and insanity.

The entry for the 8th May shows Harker aware of a wider reader as he expresses fear that he has been writing in too much detail, but then immediately ratchets up the suspense by claiming he is "glad" that he has noted all down. The sense of unease about the "strange" experiences is repeated. The threat is as yet undefined but Harker does express a wish " *I were safe out of it*". He tries his best to conquer his fears with logic. He blames his feelings on the disruption of staying up all night to talk. Even though this is a written record, there is a broken sentence reflecting intense emotion as he tries to voice his fears; "*I fear am myself the only living soul within the place*". The implicit recognition of the Count's supernatural nature is countered by Harker's attempt to "*be prosaic so far as facts can be*". He battles with himself and what he terms an imagination "*run riot*".

The journal relates an incident when shaving. Count Dracula has entered the room and despite the shaving mirror showing the room

"*there was no reflection of him in the mirror!...no sign of a man in it, except myself*".

The shock leads Harker to cut himself and the Count becomes furious, although turns quiet when he sees Jonathan's crucifix. The count warns him blood is dangerous and breaks the mirror, " *a foul bauble of man's vanity*". Harker's first reaction is annoyance, as he has no way to see himself shave.

The journal returns to recording a traveller's experience as Jonathan notes the magnificent view provided by the castle being on a "*terrific precipice*" over a "*deep rift*" and "*deep gorges*". Even here, the adjectives do suggest a large scale which can unsettle. The sublime beauty no longer distracts him. Harker turns inwards and is frustrated that there are "*Doors, doors, door everywhere, and all locked and bolted* ". He feels there are secrets behind this and repeats his dismay that the castle is a "*veritable prison*", with him a "*prisoner*".

Chapter 3

As in the previous chapter, Harker's journal entry travels across the chapter division, giving a sense of an outpouring of emotion. He returns to the realisation that he is imprisoned and notes his initial panic as he rushed around looking for an escape "*as a rat does in a trap*". He then becomes helpless and quiet when he acknowledges the Count has imprisoned him. In a spirit of 'self-help' he rallies himself and reasons he can either be made a baby by his own fear or use his brains to work out a plan.

The aspiring gentleman in Harker can still comment on the oddness that the Count seems to be doing the household chores and there is a sudden realisation that Dracula was also the driver of the coach. This increases Jonathan's fears as he knows he can control the wolves. His more reasoned mind than moves to the knowledge that the crucifix seems to help, although he cannot rationalise this. His initial plan is to encourage Dracula to talk more about his plans in order to find information to aid his escape. This element is borrowed from the mystery genre, as Harker plans to question the Count carefully, so as "*not to awake his suspicion*". Mastery and control are a key aspect of Dracula's nature. He refers to Jonathan's employer as his 'master' and often speaks in an "*imperious way*".

Dracula as feudal aristocrat

The journal is updated at midnight. Dracula is proud of his roots as a Boyar and stresses "the pride of his house and name is his own pride". He speaks like a king, using third person to speak of himself (also known as 'The Royal We'- you may notice the Queen also does this today). Stoker chooses to repeat certain images. Dracula says his ethnic group of Szekelys emerged from "*the whirlpool of European races*". There are also repeated images of flame and blood. He claims links to Attila the Hun, "*whose blood is in these veins*". It is a long and impassioned speech. For Dracula, blood and legacy is everything; "*Blood is too precious a thing in these days of dishonourable peace*". It is interesting to note that as Dracula asserts his masculine bloodline, Harker makes a link to the Arabian nights, casting himself in the feminine role.

> **Vlad Tepes (Vlad the Impaler) as Dracula?**
>
> *This chapter alludes to potential historical models for Stoker's Dracula. Calling himself a voivode, Dracula may recall the figure of Vlad III of Wallachia (1456-1462), known as Vlad the Impaler. Dracula is considered to be a likely derivative of Drac, Romanian for dragon or devil. Dracula himself claims ethnic ties with a number of conquering figures and races.*
>
> *It is important to note that recent academic study on the text draws on Stoker's draft notes, indicating that the naming of the character and setting of Transylvania occurred very late in the writing process. While links can be made to Vlad III of Wallachia, there is just as much evidence to be found in the Irish tales and superstitions Stoker grew up with, including the link between the name Dracula and the Gaelic **dreach-fhoula**, which translates as 'bad' or 'tainted blood'.*

There is a significant gap in the journal for such a pedantic book keeper and it jumps ahead to the 12th May. Suspense is sustained by the wish to rely on verified "*facts*", itself suggesting what follows may be hard to believe. The Count makes a mysterious request regarding the possibility of having multiple solicitors, as he does not wish any one company to have the power of knowledge over him. Harker does not Dracula's intelligence in legal matters.

Harker is instructed to write some letters - the Count will have "*no refusal*". It is just at this point that he sees "*the sharp, canine teeth lying over the red underlip*".

Harker makes use of shorthand as a way of keeping his communication private. The Count has claimed a victory, instructing Harker on what to write. This does not dissuade Jonathan from searching through Dracula's paperwork. This investigation adds to the mystery and suspense. Jonathan is warned to sleep only in his rooms. The result of doing otherwise is indicated in a sinister mime 'washing his hands' of Jonathan.

Bram Stoker's Dracula: A Study Guide for A Level

The next journal entry suggests Jonathan had looked south to freedom. He describes the view with positive lexis, noting the "*soft yellow moonlight*" and the "*velvety blackness*" of the shadows. He secretly observes the count and is horrified to see Dracula crawl down the wall "*just as a lizard*". Once again he confirms that we are in the realm of the supernatural:

"*What manner of man is this, or what manner of creature is it in the semblance of man?*"

It was this action that terrified the contemporary readers as much as the blood draining, which was a familiar characteristic from earlier vampire narratives.

Dracula as mystery story

This part of the narrative owes much to mystery and adventure genres, as Harker uses his limited time alone to explore a means of escape. There is a form of power struggle between Harker and Dracula. Harker takes some satisfaction in rebelling against Dracula's instructions to stay in certain parts of the castle. He finds what seem to be ladies' quarters, and as he updates his journal, he imagines himself to be sitting at the table where love letters were once written. He breaks this unusual moment of empathy with a belief that his shorthand may help transmit his views without Dracula's knowledge - "*It is the nineteenth century up-to-date with a vengeance*".

By the 16th May journal entry Harker is questioning his own sanity. He wishes to resist a loss of senses "*if, indeed, I be not made already*". Suspense is created when he suggests there are "*foul things*" in the castle which make the Count "*least dreadful*". In the midst of his terror, he feels the process of writing a diary gives him "*repose*". As the narrative develops, a number of characters will make similar remarks about the restorative and calming qualities of record keeping.

Voluptuous (OED) of a woman.

1. Attractive in a sexual way. Curvaceous and sexually attractive.

2. Relating to or characterised by luxury or sensual pleasure

from Late Middle English/ Old French.

The reader is deep in a conventional Gothic mystery as Harker admits that he has ignored Dracula's warnings and found himself drifting to sleep in the ladies' chambers. He attributes the events he now describes to a dream. The text elides the boundaries between sleep and waking; Jonathan claims it is sanity and madness blurred.

Three women appear - two with similar looks and eyes, and a "*fair*" vampire with "*golden*" hair and "*sapphire*" eyes; "*all three had brilliant white teeth that shone like pearls against the ruby of their voluptuous lips*". The suggestiveness of the pre-modifier "*voluptuous*" transforms into an erotic attraction to the strange women, as Harker confesses "*a wicked, burning desire that they would kiss me with those red lips*".

In an inversion of the Victorian melodrama, it is Harker who is the submissive victim of their attentions. He seems hypnotised by them and cannot react, even when he recognised an offensive tinge in breath "*as one smells in blood*". The tone shifts to one of horror, as the angelic appearance of the fair woman does not stop her "*gloating*". There is horror at the "*voluptuousness*" as she approaches him licking her lips "*like an animal*". The colour red is evident in her "*scarlet lips*" and "*red tongue*", conveying the ambiguity of danger and passion in the scene. The woman's teeth touch his throat as the Count intervenes "*in a storm of fury*". The women respond with an animal rage.

The Count's wrath and fury is like "*the demons of the pit*". The hellish imagery is compounded by his "*blazing eyes*" which seemed to emanate a "*red light...as is the flames of hell fire blazed behind them*". He hurls the fair woman away from Jonathan and keeps the others at bay as he has done with the wolves. He warns them "*This man belongs to me!*" He chastises the women and insists "*Yes I too can love*". Some modern critics have interpreted this as a romantic possession of Harker and have seen it as an expression of same-sex desire. It can be countered that in terms of mastery Dracula needs Jonathan to perfect his assimilation as a gentleman.

Horror is compiled when the women leave with a "*dreadful bag*", believed to contain a living child. They disappear, yet Jonathan cannot see a door. His mind is overwhelmed by the experience and he loses consciousness.

Chapter 4

This provides a continuation of the day's diary. Jonathan recounts waking up in his own bed, uncertain if the women were a nightmare or delusion. His rational side takes over and he notes that the way his clothes are folded suggest the Count did indeed carry him to his bed. There is explicit awareness that the women wanted to "*suck...blood*". Evil has fed on innocence as the female vampires feed on local children.

The entry for the 18th May shows that Harker can be brave and fearless. He returns to the forbidden rooms to investigate. The following day the Count instructs him to write and pre-date a series of letters, claiming it will help him write to friends and family when there is an "*uncertain post*". Harker calmly recognised that the Count is planning to kill him and the date on the final letter gives him the date of his death. Tension is heightened at the end of May, when he tries to bribe the Szgany men in the courtyard to post his letters, and they take these directly back to Dracula, who proceeds to lock Jonathan into his rooms.

The journal of the 31st May reveals that the Count has taken his belongings and no longer stays to talk. Harker deduces that the County is posing as him in the village. A woman comes to the castle demanding her child - it is clear that Jonathan is seen as the kidnapper. Dracula sends a wolf to kill her. The doubling of Dracula and Harker is a reminder of the liminal states. Likewise, the women appear as specks of dust in the moonlight. Harker is aware that he is falling under a spell and fights to maintain consciousness.

By the 25th June Harker still has hope. He notes the daytime causes fear to dissolve. He calls for the "*courage of the day*". Jonathan has no obvious exit so will imitate the Count and try to crawl down the wall. He makes it to Dracula's rooms and he does find heaps of gold and jewellery from many countries in this room. He finds a tunnel and has the courage to investigate, despite the "*deathly, sickly odour*". He reaches a ruined chapel and the horror is increased as he finds the Count in one of the tomb-like boxes. The Count seems suspended between life and death as cheeks and lips appear red.

Harker's escape

The journal reaches the 29th June, the date of the last letter and the beginning of the Count's final plan. Harker wishes to kill Dracula by "*lethal weapon*" but has recognised that he is supernatural and that nothing made;

> "*by man's hand would have any effect on him*".

The Count says they must part and seems to exchange pleasantries as he "*hopes that I shall see more of you at Castle Dracula*". Harker senses doom and threat beneath the "*sweet courtesy*". Jonathan insists on being able to leave, at which point Dracula opens the door to show the howling wolves have gathered. He seems to enjoy Harker's suffering, opening the door "*with a smile that Judas in hell might be proud of*". Dracula has betrayed humans and showed his monstrosity. A short time later, he overhears the Count warn the women "*Tonight he is mine...*"

Harker has survived to the 30th June and begins to pray as he desperately seeks escape. There is further horror to come. As Jonathan finds Dracula in his box he is astounded to see "*his youth had been half-restored*". He seems to have gorged on blood and Harker's disgust is evident;

> "*He lay like a filthy leech, exhausted with his repletion*".

Once again, Harker looks for a key. He is spurred to survive and escape by envisioning a London where Dracula may be able to feed and "*create a new and ever-widening circle of semi-demons*". Harker now fuelled with "terrible desire" to destroy Dracula. It should be noted that often Harker's desire overcomes his rational side and now he strikes violently with a spade. The chilling outcome is that Dracula's eyes open and stare with "*basilisk horror*". While Jonathan has caught Dracula's forehead with the spade and he still remains unconscious he does seem to have a "*grin of malice*". Harker's new horror is that he is left alone in the castle with the terrible women who are not like Mina, but "*devils of the Pit!*"

While seemingly prosaic, Jonathan does remember to take some gold to fund his escape. The novel does seem to support capitalism, as later in the text money is required to pursue the Count back across Europe. Harker re-traces the journey down the castle wall and suggests that he has no fear of falling, as if he dies he will welcome "*God's mercy*" and death would allow him to "*sleep, as a man*".

> **TASK: Close Reading – The threat to masculinity**
>
> How does Stoker create a sense of horror in the description of Jonathan Harker's encounter with the vampire women?
>
> You should consider:
> - The actions and reactions of Harker
> - The attitudes of the women
> - The way in which this extract relates to other parts of the novel.

3.2 " Tell me all the news when you write....": Chapters 5-7

In this section we will;

- Consider how language and imagery convey writer's intentions in Dracula
- Evaluate the methods employed by Stoker to convey the patterns of natural speech and thought processes
- To show understanding of how Stoker's choice of form, structure and language shapes meanings.

Chapter 5

Jonathan Harker's journal ended with a goodbye to Mina. Chapter 5 opens with Mina's letter to her friend Lucy. The following chapters provide perspectives on their friendship and female experience.

The letter is dated 9th May. Stoker employs non-chronological narrative, or interlacing, to enable readers to view the events from various perspectives. As we begin to read Mina's letter, we are aware Harker has been in peril. The date on this letter places it concurrent with Jonathan's first week at the Count's castle.

Social communication

We learn Mina works as an assistant schoolmistress. She longs to "*talk freely*" with her friend. She is working hard on a number of skills to help her become an assistant for Jonathan. She mentions working on stenography and with a typewriter. Like Jonathan, she can uses shorthand, and appreciates the ability to be able to encode personal thoughts in letters and diaries. She finds it liberating and employs it "*wherever I feel inclined*". The practice of journalist keeping is regarded as a useful exercise for aspiring lady journalists. Mina is an industrious woman who embodies the ethos of 'self-help'. She is self-denigrating in her letter to Lucy, referring to her skills development as "*little plans*".

THE 1895 - MODEL - - - - - DENSMORE TYPEWRITER.

Do you want to save time, worry and expense?
Do you want an up-to-date typewriter that challenges the world to produce its equal in modern improvements and conveniences?
The new 1895-model Densmore is a triumph, and stands to-day BEST the world over.
A special descriptive circular in exchange for your name.

UNITED TYPEWRITER AND SUPPLIES COMPANY,
85, Queen Street, Cheapside, London, E.C.

In a sharp contrast to the horrific and extreme events described in Harker's journal, the exchange between Mina and Lucy seems to be typical of romantic fiction. Mina asks Lucy to confirm rumours of *"a tall, handsome, curly-haired man"*. The tone is light and playful. Lucy seems less adept at written interchanges, confessing *"I have nothing to tell you. There is nothing to interest you"*. She then goes on to detail a busy social life of walks, visits to galleries and rides in the park. She reveals her handsome strange is a man named Mr Holmwood, who gets on well with her mother. She then proposes a man who would have been *"perfect for Mina"* due to his intellect, if she had not already been engaged to Jonathan.

Lucy dwells on the doctor (who we later find is Dr Seward) and his unsettling habit of looking directly into your face. She prides herself on being hard to read and *"a tough nut to crack"*. The reference to reading faces recalls beliefs in phrenology and physiognomy which link to Jonathan's observations on the Count and his lack of reflection. Mirrors are symbolic in the text. In asking Mina is she has looked in a mirror she is perhaps inviting the reader to see themselves reflected in the story. Lucy's letter does may occasional use of slang, a sign of familiarity with Mina, who has been a childhood friend. The exchanges between Lucy and Mina present an idealised portrait of Victorian womanhood.

Lucy confesses love for 'him', although she has mentioned more than one gentleman in her letter. There follows a second letter from Lucy dated 24th May in which she has much to report, having received three marriage proposals in one day. She betrays her youth when she imagines other girls now wanting six proposals in competition. There is a trace of irony as Lucy protests *"Some girls are so vain!"* before continuing with her recount. Lucy may be seen as having a degree of vanity, despite criticising that in others. She seems to mean no harm, as she looks forward to the near future when her and Mina can be "old married women" together.

Much of the letter provides details of the various proposals. The doctor, named as Seward, was *"cool...but...nervous"*. Lucy gently mocks his nerves, recalling how he almost sat on his hat and played with his medical lancet. The introduction of this surgical needle provides an image which will foreshadow the later transfusions and staking Lucy is subjected to. Seward is shown to have admirable qualities and behaves like a gentleman, asking to remain friends when she rejects his proposal.

Lucy expresses sorrow that she has had to hurt her rejected suitors. She continues by describing the proposal from Quincey Morris, a visiting Texan who shares his adventures. While he is fond of slang, Lucy is careful to note that he is educated and mannered, and she regards him as *"young and fresh"* in comparison to his English peers.

Stoker has Morris employ a striking metaphor in his proposal, as he asks Lucy if she will *"hitch up alongside of me and let us go down the long road together"*. As with Seward, he is dignified in rejection and calls her an honest woman. If she truly loves another, he asks only to be her *"faithful friend"*. Lucy admires Quincey's *"brave eyes"* and does award him with a kiss when he points out she has not become engaged yet.

The continued discussion of marriage provides an echo of the vampire brides. Morris pleading for a kiss may recall Harker's attraction to the 'red lips'. It should be recalled that the kiss formed a significant bond between people and it is the vampire's 'kiss' that reproduces the species. Lucy confesses that if she "*were free*" she would accept Morris. Connections are made between love and freedom, with social convention positioning marriage as a form of slavery or compromise.

At this point Lucy makes a rather shocking suggestion in her letter, which she quickly retracts:

"*Why can't they let a girl marry three men...But this is heresy...*".

There is a little irony in Lucy then glossing and spending little time on the successful proposal, from Arthur Holmwood. It is perhaps her genuine feeling for him which keeps her from trivialising an important moment, as she expresses joy at finding "*such a lover, such a husband, and such a friend*".

Dr. Seward's Phonograph

We have not read Mina's replies but now switch to a different form of text as information is provided from Dr.Seward's diary. In another reference to the new technology of the day, Seward records his daily thoughts on a phonograph, an early form of recording and playback equipment relying on wax cylinders. While the information has been written down, there is a sense that this is a record of spontaneous thoughts and the use of minor sentences and breaks in syntax create this impression.

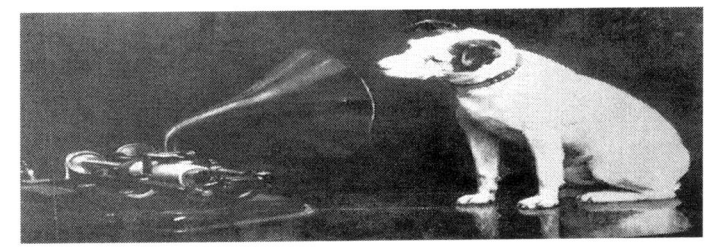

The first recording is the 25th May. It is an example of the interlacing narrative in that the reader may realise this is the day after he has proposed to Lucy and faced rejection. Seward seeks to recover through work.

The reader learns he works in an asylum. His focus is a nameless patient, as he endeavours to get to "*the heart of his misery*". Seward is reflexive and is aware his questions to his patient verged on the cruel. He does not want to encourage madness and would avoid as "*the mouth of hell*". He knows that "*Hell has its price!*".

As with Harker's travelogue, Seward's diary mimics case notes as he describes Renfield. His register is both technical and philosophical. In places his journal is circular and hard to understand. This reflects his thought process.

Seward's journal is interwoven with other texts. A short letter from Quincey Morris to Arthur Holmwood shows friendship between Lucy's previous suitors. His informal shortening to "*dear Art*" and reference to all three men knowing each other suggests homosocial bonding, formed by their travel together. The imagery of the campfire establishes a site for male friendship. Morris is frank as he suggests it will be a chance to heal and toast the new engagements. Stoker aims to create a sense of his Texan dialect and idioms. There is ironic foreshadowing as Morris references the Bible and ladies waiting with lamps, yet Lucy will soon be in a hellish union with Dracula.

Holmwood's response by telegram is equally warm-hearted and the enthusiastic wish that he should "*count me in every time*" suggests a deep friendship between the men which will be demonstrated in the course of the novel. The reader perhaps wonders what Arthur might have to say that would "*make your ears tingle*".

Chapter 6

The narrative is now presented through Mina Murray's journal. This is dated the 24th July and has been written in Whitby. As with Jonathan on his business trip, Mina has researched her surroundings and is conversant with the history of Whitby Abbey. She has chosen a churchyard to admire the view, finding it a calm place to sit and write. Mina shares Harker's powers of observation as she outlines the geography of the town and harbour spread before her.

It is here the "*old man*" is introduced. Stoker includes 'eye dialect' to indicate the colloquial vocabulary and pronunciation of the local area. The man quickly debunks the popular legends Mina asks about, saying they are for the titillation of day trippers. He goes on to wonder why other locals would bother telling lies. Mina sees him as source of information on whale fishing - he leaves for tea. The old man's dialogue is recorded by Mina and is based on a wide range of dialect words which Stoker collected when on holiday in Whitby himself.

WHITBY ABBEY, THE CHOIR.

Mr Swales

In the entry for the 1st August Mina emphasises Lucy's sweetness and prettiness. The two women continue to meet with the old sailors to discuss local legends. The cynical Mr Swales scoffs at ridiculous superstitions, listing in local dialect and dismissing all as "*air-blebs...all invented by parsons*". He moves on to a criticism of the lies people tell on tombstones. He highlights that it is a whaling and fishing town like Whitby, many of the tombstones decorate empty graves, as these lives were lost at sea. He also mocks those headstones declaring sacred memories when the men were unloved in life. There is a sense of the gravestone providing immortality.

Mina confesses in her diary that she misunderstands a number of his words but gets the gist, and is able to guess, as when she figures that "*kirkgarth*" means 'church'. Mr Swales is not sentimental as he insists that many "*bones lie in the Greenland seas above*". Mina attempts to correct him on his unusual belief that the dead need to be reunited with their tombstones to get to Heaven. She suggests a gravestone may be designed to please relatives. Swales also scoffs this idea - when Lucy mentions a "*sorrowing mother*" he argues the woman is "*a hell-cat*" and that her son committed suicide to get away from her, and was happy to go to his death.

Lucy is upset to find her favourite spot is directly over a suicide. Mr Swales tries to reassure her, sure that Geordie would be glad "*to have so trim a lass sittin' on his lap*". Lucy is calmed and when Swales leaves is excited to tell Mina about her wedding plans, reminding her that she has not heard from Jonathan.

Mina returns to the graveyard alone at nine as the evening lights are coming on. She tries to focus on the view. There is a future contrast between Mina's twilight reflections and Lucy's later nocturnal sleepwalks.

> **TASK: Minor Characters**
>
> **What is the significance of Mr Swales in the larger narrative?**
> You should consider:
> - Aspects of language and imagery relating to character
> - Links to larger themes

Renfield as case study

The narrative switched to Dr Seward's diary, although this is not chronological as it is dated 5th June. This entry presents a case study of Renfield and his "*selfishness, secrecy and purpose*". Seward wants to identify his patient's motivation. He presents a series of entries where he notes the odd pets have developed from flies to spiders to sparrows. On the 1st July he witnesses Renfield eating a fly and discovers a notebook where he seems to be keeping a tally of the 'lives' he is ingesting. By mid-July Seward refuses his patient's request for a kitten, resulting in a fierce look which reveals an "*undeveloped homicidal maniac*". On the 20th July feathers and blood in Renfield's cell are soon followed by evidence that he has eaten the birds raw. Seward seems elated rather than concerned as he has coined a term for his patient - *zoophagous*, or life-eating maniac. He almost admires Renfield's experimental model, comparing it to vivisection, a controversial practice at the time of the novel (and indeed still so today).

Zoophagous

A life-eating maniac

An adaptation of a term used by the Greek Historian Herodotus;

Androphagoi; or 'Man-eaters' to describe a tribe of cannibals.

Seward thinks of his own career advancement. If he could find the 'key' to Renfield he might advance the field of psychology. He coins the term '*zoophagous*' and hopes to become an expert in this field. He knows this investigation could corrupt him and knows he "*may be tempted*". Seward may be seen here as having a desire for mastery which echoes Dracula. Who should society fear - the monster or the ambitious scientist pushing ethical boundaries?

Seward can rationalise his study for a good enough cause and expresses a belief that he has "*an exceptional brain*". He feels this could be applied to Renfield, who has shown a degree of reasoning and the ability to start again;

"*How well the man reasoned, lunatics always do within their own scope*".

Seward ends his recording with a direct reference to his disappointment about Lucy, seeing work as a "*cure*" for his heartache.

> **TASK: Minor Characters**
>
> What do we learn about Renfield from Dr Seward?
> How does Stoker create a sense of threat in Renfield's requests?

The narrative once again is provided through Mina Murray's diary and returns to 26th July. She has received a letter from Hawkins, Harker's employer. As with Jonathan, she uses her journal to calm her own anxiety, stating "*it soothes me to express myself here*". The couple are linked by their vocabulary. As she reads the brief letter, which the reader knows has been dictated by Dracula, she feels deeply "*uneasy*".

Lucy has worried Mina by starting to sleepwalk again. Mina has had to lock Lucy in to their bedroom. There is a sense of financial disparity and a difference in social class between Lucy and Mina. While Lucy has grand plans for her marital home, Mina reflects:

"*Jonathan and I will start in life in a very simple way, and shall have to try to make both ends meet*".

The entry for the 27th July repeats that Mina is "*uneasy*" about Jonathan while Lucy continues to sleepwalk. Mina is "*nervous and wakeful*" herself. Lucy does not seem to be suffering from lack of sleep and Mina even suggests she is "*a trifle stouter*" and have cheeks of "*a lovely rose-pink*". It is a mystery how she can lap sleep yet not seem anaemic.

On the 3rd August Mina is now convinced something has happened with Jonathan. She senses a storm. Lucy now attempts to escape the room and look for the key, although the sleepwalking has decreased. The entry for the 6th August fears that something "*dreadful*" has happened to Jonathan. She distracts herself by trying to get to know Whitby better, asking Swales and others to teach her how to predict the weather. The sound carrying over the sea is "*like some passage of doom*". Mina notes that Swales has drastically changed, repeatedly referring to him as a "*poor old*" man. He seems regretful of his earlier comments about gravestones and explains his fear of dying. He warns that there is something on the wind that "*looks, and tastes, and smells like death*". He blesses her and says goodbye. At the same time it is noted that a "*strange ship*" is moving bizarrely in the bay.

Chapter 7: Making the news

The chapter opens with a newspaper cutting which has been pasted into Mina's journal. Named as *The Dailygraph* and dated the 8th August, it is a local journalist's record of an unusual event in a storm. The report begins by stressing that it had been a beautiful day, with Whitby full of day-trippers. The article moves backwards and forwards in time as the "*dead calm*" of midnight is broken by a booming sound as the wind "*roared like thunder*". There is use of personification, as the sky trembles under "*the footsteps of the storm*". There is a sense of panic as the searchlight in used and the fishing boats rush in. A "*mass of dark mist*" was noted. A ship crashes into the harbour, when it is gruesomely revealed that a dead man is lashed to the wheel and the ship was steered "*by the hand of a dead man!*". A large dog was seen leaping off the ship and running up the East pier. Strangely, the dead captain has bound his hands to the wheel with a crucifix. The text develops themes of the power of the supernatural and human imagination. In the ghoulish corpse of the captain there is a blurring of the boundaries between the living and the dead.

Whitby and liminality

In Whitby the sea meets land and the living meet the dead. Mina has many of her conversations with Swales in the graveyard. The traditional Legend of the White Lady links to St. Hilda, said to appear on stormy nights to guide sailors to shore. There is the uncanny fact that many of the graves lie empty as the bones of the sailors are lost at sea. This is a fitting location for the sleepwalking Lucy to encounter Dracula, as she remains in state between waking and sleeping, and soon hangs between life and death.

The next entry is dated the 9th August, and would appear to be a follow up story in the local paper. It is revealed the ship was a Russian schooner travelling from Varna. It is named the Demeter, which creates link with the myth of the woman bound to seek her daughter in the underworld. The correspondent has observed mould wooden boxes - the reader may already be starting to make a link to the activity seen at Count Dracula's castle. The story seems to return to the mundane as a Whitby solicitor takes care of the cargo and there is a search for the missing dog with the newly established SPCA (Society for the Protection of Cruelty to Animals). A more sinister note returns when it is reported that the coal merchant's guard dog has been found with its throat turn out and stomach split, as if by a wild animal.

The next entry is a copy of the Captain's log, which has been shared by the Trade Inspector. The text is framed as recording the 'mania' of the captain. In the earlier entries to the captain's log, he detailed how they had to pay off various port authorities with a *backsheesh*, or bribe. This suggests there is something illicit about what is being carried. He notes members of the crew begin to go missing. The men are "*scared*" and have an uncanny sense that "*something*" is on board. There is talk of a strange man who cannot be found. The ship encounters a series of storms and the captain has noted that as the second man disappears beyond the Bay of Biscay they have "*four days in hell*". His crew are beyond fear as one by one they go missing. Reduced to the captain and his Mate, the Mate fears a "*tall...thin...ghastly pale*" man. The Captain assumes that the Mate has lost his sanity and is behind the disappearances, but fear remains after the Mate jumps ship. The Captain ties himself to the wheel, with a vague fear about "*this fiend or monster*". The ultimate fate of the captain and the reasons behind the death remain a "*mystery of the sea*", as the people of Whitby bury him as a hero.

Weathering the Storm

The chapter concludes with Mina's diary entry for the 8th August, when she gives her version of the storm. Storms are primal; an archetypal symbol of chaos, which is emphasised in the picture overleaf.

Mina also discusses the uncanny nature of Lucy's sleepwalking noting that:

" *as soon as her will is thwarted in any physical way, her intention, if there be any, disappears, and she yields herself almost exactly to the routine of her life*".

The 10th August sees the funeral of the sea captain. Mina notes a dog howled throughout the ceremony and Lucy is restless throughout the day, and the final shock was to discover that their companion Mr Swales was found dead on their

Bram Stoker's Dracula: A Study Guide for A Level

'seat' at the tombstone with a broken neck, having fallen back over it with a look of horror. It is recalled that this is a suicide seat and that God will forsake suicides. Victorians also found this taboo. The harmless bench has become a site for evil. The women are upset and Mina plans to distract from this and to discourage Lucy's sleepwalking by taking her on a tiring walk along the cliff path to Robin Hood's Bay.

TASK: Genre and Style

What is the effect of the inclusion of a newspaper report at the start of the chapter?

How does Stoker use the ship's log of the Demeter to build suspense?

You should consider:

- How each text type may create a sense of immediacy
- The ways in which Stoker presents information to the reader

---

Bram Stoker's Dracula: A Study Guide for A Level

3.3 "So far there is much that is strange": Chapters 8-16

In this section we will;

- *Consider how language and imagery convey writer's intentions in Dracula*
- *Evaluate the methods employed by Stoker to convey the patterns of natural speech and thought processes*
- *To show understanding of how Stoker's choice of form, structure and language shapes meanings.*

Chapter 8

Victorians and sleepwalking

The desire in life was for patterns of order and authority over self. Earlier forms of hypnosis such as mesmerism were rejected as there were real fears about the actions someone could commit when under the influence of others. There was a need to map seemingly autonomous and automatic behaviours. Sleepwalking was viewed with suspicion as the brain seemed 'switched off' and a person could become their own 'double', enacting dark desires. Sleepwalking was regarded as a real threat to social order and personal well-being. The threat was intensified in a female sufferer, as their purity was also considered under threat.

Mina is precise with her journal and notes the time as 11.00pm. She sees her diary as a "*duty*". She describes the "*severe tea*" shared with Lucy as Robin Hood's Bay. Both women are disparaging about the 'New Woman' saying they have eaten to rival this stereotype of the independent and free-thinking female. Lucy's health appears to be improving, although Mina still has worries about Jonathan.

Mina writes late as she is unable to sleep but has a sudden realisation that Lucy's bed is empty. Initially searching for Lucy in the house, she has to venture into the town at 1.00am, hoping to find that Lucy has been sleepwalking to a familiar place. Mina tries their graveyard seat, over a mile from the house, and in the bright moon sees a "*snowy white*" figure with a long, black shape behind it, which seems to become human with a white face and red eyes.

Mina cannot process what she has seen but it would seem to be an attack on Lucy in the vulnerable state between waking and sleeping, much as Harker experienced in the castle.

Mina braves this scene and finds Lucy in a state of sleep with laboured breath. Mina fears she has pierced her throat with a pin, a confirmation to the reader of what has truly happened. Even in the middle of this extraordinary discovery, Mina is mindful enough to protect their reputations, lending Lucy her shoes and using mud to appear as though she also has footwear to avoid a scandal of two young women out in town in the middle of the night. Returning to the house, she blames her clumsy use of the pin on the marks on Lucy's throat. Lucy claims to feel better but Mina sleeps with the key to the room. She wakes to see a bat outside the window.

The entrance to the 14th August records Lucy's unsettled mind, as she compares the sunset to "*his red eyes again!*". There seems to be a dark figure on their favoured seat, but Mina decides it is an illusion caused by the reflection and refraction of light. Lucy is becoming thin and drawn, and goes to bed early. As Mina sets off on a walk alone, she looks back to see Lucy with what appears to be a bird.

Lucy has been transformed by Dracula. She has assumed what she has experienced is the product of dreams, yet recognises it felt real. She is "*not herself*" at sundown and as with the sleepwalking self would seem to develop the more liberal sexuality of the New Woman in place of earlier innocence.

Lucy's mother also confides in Mina. She informs her that she is dying of a heart condition but does not want to worry her already sick daughter.

Two days later, Mina's diary entry of the 17th August notes that Lucy is deteriorating, as the "*roses in her cheeks are fading*". Despite her weakness, Mina finds her leaning out the window.

> **TASK: Narrative Style**
>
> **How does Stoker make use of Gothic imagery in Mina's recount of Lucy's sleepwalking?**
>
> You could consider setting, atmosphere, and the descriptions of characters and actions.

The narrative is then interspersed with a copy of a solicitor's letter and response relating to the movement of boxes from Whitby to London. The confirmation of the arrival of the cargo in London is the 21st August.

Returning to Mina's journal and the 18th August, Lucy appears to sleep calmly. She talks to Mina about her memories of the night she was found at the graveyard. She remembers dogs howling and something "*long and dark with red eyes*". She was overcome with sensations remembered as "*very sweet and very bitter*", comparing her "*agonizing feeling*" to an earthquake.

News of Jonathan

Mina's attempts to catalogue Lucy's illness are interrupted with some news of Jonathan Harker. She received it on the 19th August and discovers he is ill in a convent in Budapest. The letter from Sister Agatha is dated 12th August and hints that Harker has had some dreadful worries. Mina makes plans to go to him, nurse him and marry as soon as possible.

The narrative now presents Dr Seward's diary, also for the 19th August. He has found his patient Renfield highly excitable, as he repeatedly shouts "*The master is at hand*". Seward suspects a form of religious mania. His journal also reveals that he still thinks of Lucy and has been drugging himself to get to sleep. On the evening of the 19th he did not medicate himself and Renfield attempted an escape. There is a parallel to Lucy - while the text refers to Renfield being "*naked*" it is likely he has also ventured out in his sleeping tunic. Both have escaped from a seemingly secure room.

Seward tracks his patient to the grounds of Carfax Abbey. The reader is aware this is the new home of Harker's Count Dracula. There is a struggle to contain and return Renfield. Renfield articulates what he has seen. He has been summoned by his 'Master' and makes references to John the Baptist. Seward diagnosed religious mania. In a text with a focus on the monstrous, Renfield may be seen as a subversion of a disciple waiting for his anti-Christ, Dracula.

The reader may have paid attention to the dates, and noticed that Lucy has peaceful sleep on the 17th and 18th of August, while Renfield's escape takes place on the 18th into the 19th. This interlacing of the plot suggests that there is one influence over both characters. They are unaware but the reader may begin to make connections. This is a form of dramatic irony found elsewhere in the narrative when Mina is left alone at the asylum.

Chapter 9

The reader notes the letter from 24th August is addressed from Mina Harker to Lucy Westenra. She is now married to Jonathan. Her first impression of him in the convent was he was " *a wreck of himself*". The nuns caring or him repeatedly make the sign of the cross and will not reveal what he has said, but assure Mina it was the ravings of a sick man. There are hints his tale was "*great and terrible*", involving "*no mortal*". Mina shows immediate relief it has nothing to do with another woman. Jonathan is said to have 'brain fever'. He passes Mina his journal, asking her not to tell him if she reads it.

The Harkers marry while Jonathan is still bed-ridden. Mina has wrapped his unread journal in a ribbon as a present symbolising their trust. She ends her letter with a typical wish of good luck for Lucy's married life "*please Almighty God*".

There is a reply from Lucy dated the 20th August. Still at Whitby, she seems to be in good cheer, assuring Mina that she sleeps well and has "*an appetite like a cormorant*". Arthur has joined her in Whitby and they plan to marry on the 28th September.

The text returns to Dr Seward's diary of the 20th August, the day after Renfield's 'escape'. Renfield is quiet and vows not to hurt him. He is not interested in having a kitten anymore. Seward observes Renfield is violent by day and subdued at night. Like Lucy, he varies in mood between dawn and dusk. Lucy has physical changes while Renfield's affect his mental state. As an experiment, Seward leaves an escape route to see where Renfield has been going. Renfield stays in his cell so the rules are relaxed at some times of day. Later that night Renfield does escape and almost kills Seward when confronted. He is calmed by the sight of a bat.

Lucy's sickness

The text provides entries from Lucy's diary. She begins a diary in the style of Mina's journal and on Mina's absence on the 24th August. She has returned to her London home and begins to dream again. On the 25th August she asks to sleep in her mother's room and is refused. Lucy records trying to stay awake, and has a memory of scratching or flapping at the window. She has a pain at her throat. She struggles to tell consciousness and unconsciousness apart as the clock strikes midnight. This is another occasion when the readers have more knowledge than the diary keepers. She is deteriorating as Dracula closes in. Her unremembered dreams are Dracula's visits.

A letter is sent from Arthur to Dr Seward on the 31st August. He has to leave Lucy's side as his father has failing health, and he asks Seward to check on Lucy as a doctor.

Seward's response on the 2nd September agrees that Lucy has changed since he has last met her. He states it is not a "*functional malady*" and notes it is unusual for her to be bloodless but not anaemic. Her blood appears normal to him and so he suggests the illness is "*mental*", and manifests in difficulties with sleeping and breathing. He is puzzled and informs Holmwood that he has sent for his old tutor Professor Van Helsing, who may be able to present a diagnosis given his specialism in obscure diseases. Seward has in effect presented the medical histories of Lucy and Renfield side by side, but is not yet in a position to note that there is a common cause.

The letter digresses into a pen portrait of Van Helsing, praises his "*open mind*", "*iron nerve*" and his "*kindliest and truest heart*". He is presented as an accomplished man of science. Seward is remembered by his old teacher for sucking gangrene out of a knife wound, incidentally inflicted by Quincey Morris in a previous encounter. There is an irony that bloodsucking forms the basis of Seward and Van Helsing's friendship.

A letter from Van Helsing suggests he is highly qualified, indicated by the "*etc. etc.*" at the end of his professional titles. Stoker alters sentence structures and syntax to reflect that English is not Van Helsing's first language. He vows to treat Lucy, "*I am already coming to you*".

Dr Seward then writes to Arthur on the 3rd September. He provides a secondary report as he was not present when Van Helsing saw Lucy. Van Helsing has asked Seward to develop his own theories. Seward promised to write up a report.

Seward returns to his diary on the 4th September. He has classified Renfield as a "*zoophagous patient*". It is noted he is restless at twelve noon, calm by five o'clock. The diary entry is made at midnight, noting Renfield's frenzy before sunset. Seward tries to formulate theories and presents a series of telegrams to Van Helsing on the 4th, 5th and 6th September. These telegrams are short and mostly positive. There is an abrupt shift in tone when a terrible change is noted on the 6th September.

Chapter 10

A communication between Seward and Holmwood dated 6th September describes the deterioration of Lucy.

Seward's diary on the 7th September makes use of Van Helsing's idiolect as Seward recounts Van Helsing's plans. Seward has been asked to keep his ideas and plans to himself, fearing the reactions of "*God's madmen too, the rest of the world*". Van Helsing still keeps his ideas to himself- he assures Seward "*Later I shall unfold to you*". He uses a complex analogy of husbandry and farming. He urges Seward to keep detailed records - "*Knowledge is stronger than memory*".

Seward describes Van Helsing's doctor's bag, with its instruments and drugs, "*the ghastly paraphernalia of our beneficial trade*". Doctors are meant to heal but there was a fear of the invasive surgical procedures being developed.

Mrs Westenra is the stereotype of delicate Victorian womanhood. She is dying and the doctors are careful not to frighten her and make her anxious about her daughter. A medical metaphor makes a comparison to nature attacking a foreign body or virus. Mrs Westenra seems detached and disassociated from events around her.

The need for blood

Lucy is now "*ghastly, chakily pale*". The red vitality of life has gone and she seems a ghost. Van Helsing has realised her "*sheer want of blood*". The ambiguity of "*want*" suggests Lucy's transformation into a vampire. Transfusions were a new and unorthodox technique at the time of writing (identification of blood types would not be secured until 1908 and the mixing of blood shown in the novel could result in blood poisoning). The transfusions create dramatic tension.

Seward has volunteered to give his blood as "*younger and stronger*". Arthur arrives and Van Helsing sees him as a specimen of "*strong young manhood*". Arthur, as Lucy's fiancée, vows that he "*would give the last drop of blood in my body for her*". Van Helsing finds a dark humour in this and informs him of the need for transfusion. Van Helsing allows Arthur to "*kiss her once before it is done*". Lucy is put under a narcotic. It is a basic model of medicine Van Helsing claims that Arthur's blood is so pure that it would not need treating. There is a symbiosis as Arthur weakens and Lucy is restored. There is a sense this is a union as Van Helsing declares Arthur "*deserves another kiss*" at the end of the transfusion. The exchange of blood is treated as an intimate act. This contrasts with Dracula's 'kiss', which is an act of violation from a conqueror. Arthur's blood is designed to give life while Dracula takes blood and hastens death.

Seward still attempts to puzzle out the case, asking Van Helsing about the marks on Lucy's throat. Seward has realised there is a link between the wound and her loss of blood. He is asked to undertake a vigil and stay awake as Lucy sleeps.

Van Helsing still chooses to keep his knowledge to himself at this stage. He leaves Seward to go to Amsterdam to research further. As Lucy is fighting sleep, she voices fears and has "*a presage of horror*". Seward returns to the asylum and a quiet Renfield.

The second night of the vigil on the 9th September sees Lucy sit up and offer to watch over Seward given that she has more energy. We switch briefly to Lucy's diary reflecting her positive cheer - "*I feel so happy tonight*". She reflects "*Arthur feels very, very close to me*" - the reader knows this could be due to the transfusion.

Colour and illness

Seward's diary on the 10th September begins with him recounting being woken by Van Helsing. They view Lucy with an "*exclamation of horror*", as she was "*horribly white*". Seward notes her gums seem drawn back from her teeth. He volunteers to participate in an immediate transfusion. Once again Lucy is sedated with morphine. Seward regards the transmission of blood as almost sacred and was moved watching

"*his own lifeblood drawn away into the veins of the woman he loves*".

There is a sense of competition as Seward notes more was taken from Arthur. Van Helsing reminds him that he has to work and warns him to not tell Arthur about this transfusion, in case he misunderstood. He recognised that Holmwood may still regard Seward as a rival.

His dreams focus on the wound and trying to puzzle out Lucy's worsened condition. Red is emphasised through imagery such as the "*crimson blush*" when conversation discusses a wife. It is interesting that her face is described as having "*excessive pallor*". Traditionally, the image of the sick heroine would be one of paleness. While Lucy is lacking blood, it seems as though her lips and cheeks are unusually red. This will become a characteristic of the vampire's victims.

Van Helsing still seems reluctant to share his theories about Lucy's illness with Seward. He encourages Seward to think of even the most fantastic reasons for her symptoms.

The entry of 11th September suggests Lucy is better. Van Helsing brings what is thought to be a bunch of flowers but then revealed to be garlic. Lucy's joking response to this is cut short when Van Helsing insists it has a "*grim purpose*". Seward is puzzled by a scientist such as Van Helsing introducing a superstition rather than using conventional medicine. Van Helsing assures them the garlic and keeping the windows shut should keep Lucy safe. Garlic has been a folklore remedy for a range of illnesses. He makes link to the Passover and hopes to mark the room to ward off the threat.

The narrative switches to Lucy's diary, dated 12th September. Lucy's voice still seems playful and affectionate as she declares "*I quite love that dear Van Helsing*", yet she confesses a fear of sleeping.

We then move to Seward's diary of the 13th September. Suspense is built as Lucy's mother reveals that she removed the garlic and opened the window to make Lucy's room less stuffy. Van Helsing reacts by breaking down "*in despair*". His language is spiritual rather than medical as he talks of losing Lucy "*body and soul*" and suggests that "all the powers of the devils" are against them. Lucy appears weak and Van Helsing begins a blood transfusion, sedating her with narcotics. The men begin a vigil over Lucy. Seward feels he is losing his grasp of reality, blaming his work in the asylum for "*beginning to tell upon my own brain*".

This jumps to Lucy's diary of the 17th September. Lucy writes of four days of peace but the reader may have already guesses what has caused the *"flapping against the windows"*.

Control of nature

A digression is provided with the inclusion of an extract from *The Pall Mall Gazette* of the 18th September. This provides an interview with a zookeeper Thomas Bilder. As in the passages with Swales, Stoker makes use of eye dialect to convey regional vocabulary and accent, in this case a Cockney dialect. The news item relates to an escaped wolf who interacts with a tall, thin man with a *"cold look and red eyes"* and *"a mouth full of sharp teeth"*. The mysterious man tells the zookeeper he has kept wolves as pets. The reader may recall Jonathan's Count and his power over wolves. The reader is reminded of Dracula's mastery over animals.

Dramatic irony is created through the interlaced narrative in this chapter, as the reader identifies the jeopardy Lucy faces ahead of the other characters. Chronology is disrupted with a return to the 17th September in Seward's diary. He has been engaged in book-keeping when Renfield escapes his cell and threatens him with a knife, attempting to lick the blood from the wound. Seward is exhausted and needs *"rest, rest, rest"*. He notes it is just as well that he is not needed at Lucy's that evening.

This entry is followed by the text from a telegram sent to Carfax on the 17th September. Van Helsing urgently asks Seward to rush to Lucy at Hillingham. The previous section lets the reader know that Seward is asleep and has missed the telegram. The failure to be with Lucy will be a crucial turning point.

Seward's diary from the morning of the 18th September notes a fear of *"horrible doom"*.

Suspense is sustained as the narrative switches perspective once again. Ominously, this section is labelled "Memorandum left by Lucy Westenra". The use of past tense suggests a negative outcome. Dated 17th September, Lucy is aware that death is approaching. She once again hears flapping at the window, and is unable to sleep, then unable to stay awake. A howl is heard outside. On investigating Lucy sees a bat before a wolf breaks through the glass of her window. Her mother tears the garlic from Lucy's neck in her panic. Lucy recalls specks caught in light which transform into a *"pillar of dust"*. She finds herself unable to move and feels under a spell. She is aware her mother is dead, perhaps from heart failure due to shock. Dogs continue to howl while a nightingale already reminds her of her mother. Lucy lays garlic on her mother's body and sends the maids for a drink to calm their nerves.

Lucy's horror builds as she finds her maids have been drugged with laudanum in the sherry. She notes floating specks in the air. The reader may recall Harker's women as Lucy finds herself *"Alone with the dead!"*

Biblical allusions in the text

Throughout the text, Stoker makes use of Biblical allusions, subverting them to suggest Dracula as an evil presence needing a strong Christian response. The description of Dracula as a pillar of dust, and Mina's later reference to him as a mist recalls Exodus, where God presented as a pillar of cloud to guide the Israelites, becoming a pillar of fire at night. Dracula would seem to invert this image. Instead of leading others to salvation, his appearance in a mist or cloud and his fiery red eyes are a sign of the potential damnation, as transformation into the un-dead jeopardises Lucy's soul and purity. Renfield is also known to directly quote the Old Testament.

Chapter 12

We return to Seward's diary on the 18th September. He now describes his arrival at Lucy's house and there is a pompous arrogance in him cursing the "*laziness*" of the servants who are slow to answer the door. His attitude increases the horror of what lies ahead.

Seward struggles to get into the house. There is urgent action as Van Helsing arrives. The men have to saw their way through the barred kitchen window. Seward is sent to rouse the maids while Van Helsing predicts "*a stand-up fight with death*". He brings Lucy back and leaves a maid with her. There is heroism when Van Helsing vows to confront "*all the devils at once...we fight him all the same*".

He argues that the transfusion must come from a man. Quincey Morris arrives, having been sent by Arthur to check Lucy's health. Van Helsing praises the offer of "*a brave man's blood*", as he once again uses morphine to sedate Lucy. The men have essentially spilled blood for Lucy's literal salvation.

Seward reads Lucy's memo and concludes that she is mad. Seward and Van Helsing arrange to certify Mrs Westenra's death to avoid a scandal while Quincey Morris is sent with a telegram to urge Arthur to visit.

When Morris talks with Seward he recalls a horse being attacked by a vampire bat. This suggests he has guessed the nature of Lucy's illness. Morris also volunteers to help keep a vigil at her bedside.

Lucy remains distraught about her mother. In her sleep she tears up the memo left the previous day. Seward returns to his role as a medical practitioner, as he observes and records differences between Lucy's sleeping and waking states. Sleep makes her look stronger. Her breathing is soft but her teeth are sharp. She seems more herself when awake. Seward predicts she is near death as Arthur is sent for.

Interlacing narratives

The reader is told they are now reading an unopened letter from Mina to Lucy dated the 17th September. Mina has been absent from these events. She explains that Jonathan's employer has left him everything in his will and they have been given his house in Exeter, with Jonathan now a partner in the firm. She notes Jonathan has had restless sleep. Mina asks Lucy about her wedding preparation.

The narrative is interrupted by the inclusion of a medical report from an unknown character Patrick Hennessey. It is written for John Seward. It details Renfield's behaviour in Seward's absence. He has sworn at the men delivering goods to Carfax Abbey next door. They retaliate by calling him a "*wild beast*". Checking on Renfield, he is suddenly calm. Within half an hour Renfield has escaped and has attacked the men moving boxes. Hennessey reports Renfield as having superhuman strength. The workmen threaten to sue for assault but hint that they can be bribed with alcohol. This becomes a theme later in the novel when Jonathan tracks down the various men helping Dracula. Hennessey is principally a record-keeper, listing the names of the men involved.

The main narrative continues with an unopened letter from Mina to Lucy. The fact the letter is unopened prepares the reader for future events. Mina writes in praise of her husband and his "*simple, noble, strong nature*". She feels Hawkins recognised this when leaving Jonathan the inheritance. She informs Lucy that she will be travelling to London for the funeral, creating anticipation of a meeting.

Seward's diary from the 20th September notes that the diary forms part of a "*resolution and habit*". These are similar to the sentiments expressed by Lucy, Harker and Mina in earlier journal entries. He expresses misery and announces himself "*sick of the world*".

Lucy's room is once again covered in garlic. It is noted that she breathes "*stertorously*", like an animal. Her teeth are once again observed as prominent. A bat strikes the window. As Seward checks the noise, Lucy throws the garlic away. Seward later notes when Lucy is awake she keeps the garlic close, yet she tears it away when she is asleep.

Seward is confused when Lucy's throat wounds disappear, yet Van Helsing declares that she is dying. Arthur is summoned but is instructed not to kiss her. Seward emphasises Lucy's "*angelic beauty*" and compares her breathing to a "*tired child's*".

A change occurs, as she is once again breathing "*stretorously*". The description indicates her changed state. Seward feels the "*soft, voluptuous voice*" is not Lucy's usual tone. She uses the imperative, demanding that Arthur kiss her. Van Helsing drags him back from her and she reacts in a spasm of rage. Lucy's voice returns to normal as she implores Van Helsing to protect Arthur - "*Oh, guard him, and give me peace!*"

In death it seems she is "*given back part of her duty*", although the young men are puzzled by Van Helsing's ominous warning:
"*It is only the beginning!*

Chapter 13

This is a continuation of Seward's diary. Arthur has to attend his father's funeral as Lucy is buried. Van Helsing looks through Lucy's papers. He reminds Seward he is also a qualified lawyer and suggests they remove any document which may refer to strange events to save her reputation with strangers. Readers may question the ethics of removing documents. Van Helsing persuades Seward that the diary, memos and letters may be put to good use.

Before her burial, Lucy's bedroom is dressed as a chapel. Seward notes she is "*lovely*" in death, suggesting there is still an emotional attachment to the woman who rejected him. This also highlights Lucy's liminal state as one of the "*un-dead*". Van Helsing places garlic and a crucifix on Lucy's mouth. Seward is horrified when Van Helsing asks him to bring post-mortem knives.

The plan seems brutal. Van Helsing suggests Lucy must be protected by cutting off her head and taking out her heart. He reminds Seward that as a surgeon he has previously taken a knife to bodies. Seward finds the plan 'monstrous' but Van Helsing remains serious as he explains that they will wait for Arthur but it must happen that evening. He will not say more but does link the extreme plan to the reason he refused Arthur a kiss from his bride -to -be.

The use of "*it*" to refer to the corpse recalls the ship's log of the Demeter, when the captain referred to the nefarious "*it*" which tormented the ship. Vampirism makes humans monstrous things. It becomes a metaphor for denying another's humanity. It also suggests that gender is fluid in these encounters - it is Jonathan who swoons with weakness, and Van Helsing who cries "*just as a woman does*" later in the narrative. Dracula's actions lead to a dissolution of boundaries and stable categories.

As Seward agrees to trust in the plan there is a further complication when they discover that a maid has stolen the crucifix, leaving Lucy exposed to attack. Arthur arrives and struggles to cope with her death. He has inherited the estate and gives permission to Van Helsing to read the letters.

There follows an extract from Mina's journal. She seems bound by etiquette, as when she is self-conscious about Jonathan holding her arm in public. She notes that Jonathan suddenly became pale on seeing

"*a tall, thin man, with a beaky nose and black moustache and pointed beard*".

Mina describes the face as "*hard and cruel and sensual*". As in descriptions of Lucy, the contrast of white and red is emphasised. Jonathan's reaction is recorded as he recoils; "*It is the man himself...he has grown young!*" Jonathan sleeps often, and Mina fears he has sustained a brain injury.

Mina is surprised to receive a telegram from Van Helsing, who is unknown to her. She discovers Lucy has been dead five days.

The men unite

Seward's diary of the 22nd September sees Arthur and Quincey re-join Seward. Seward praises Quincey Morris as a "*moral Viking*". He comments on America becoming a world power in future. Seward and Van Helsing reflect on the act of sharing blood via transfusion. Arthur, unaware that the other men have donated blood to Lucy, feels that his donation has made Lucy his wife in the eyes of God. Van Helsing has a fit of hysterics on the carriage ride. It is notable that gender stereotypes prevail, as Seward is surprised that he laughs "*just as a woman does*".

There is a digression as Van Helsing muses on the power of laughter and our lack of control of it. He personifies laughter as King Laugh;
"*He is a king and he come when and how he like*".
People will "*dance to the tune he play*", even in times of sadness or despair. It almost suggests a dance of death. In the speech he reveals he has lost a son and his wife has lost her sanity and resides in an asylum. He continues to find dark humour and a grim irony in the shared blood, calling Lucy "*a polyandrist*" and himself a bigamist. Again there is a blurring of boundaries. Catholic Church law forbids divorce and Van Helsing muses on the 'infidelity' of his blood. The 'King Laugh' speech presents Van Helsing's motivation and reminds readers he is the antithesis of Dracula.

Seward is confused by this speech. It can be argued that it is proof of social condemnation of women, as despite her affliction, Lucy is compared to a woman with many men. This also presages the descriptions of female vampires as seductive and transgressive.
Seward cannot share Van Helsing's joke and vows to finish his diary "*sadly and without hope*". He states "*Finis*".

Bram Stoker's Dracula: A Study Guide for A Level

The chapter ends with a cutting from the Westminster Gazette dated the 25th September. Under the headline "*A Hampstead Mystery*" it provides details of children disappearing, with those children who did witness describing a "*bloofer lady*", a child's attempt at '*beautiful lady*". Some of the missing were found with tears and wounds in the throat.

Chapter 14

Characters are brought together in this chapter, with a bridging of plots. The chapter begins with Mina's journal from two days earlier, the 23rd September. Despite the promise made at their wedding, she now feels she needs to read Harker's journal, disturbed by his belief that the man he has seen in London may be Dracula. Mina takes a pragmatic approach to the task, deciding to transcribe the shorthand into notes that others may read if required.

There follows a communication from Van Helsing to Mrs Harker, begging for Mina's help. He offers to travel to Exeter to discuss this with her and asks her not to tell Jonathan yet. Mina sends a telegram agreeing to the visit.

Mina's journal entry of the 25th September expresses a hope that Van Helsing may be able to "*throw light*" on Jonathan's experience. Throughout the novel images of light and darkness are presented in opposition. She knows that Van Helsing was with Lucy during her illness. She decides not to mention Jonathan's journal unless asked.

Light in the darkness

When Van Helsing confirms Jonathan's journal entries are not delusions Mina is shocked. She vows to record "*verbatim*". Record keeping becomes an important tool in challenging Dracula throughout the narrative. It is elevated to the status of scientific method.

Mina is impressed by Van Helsing and comments that his head shape is "*indicative of thought and power*". This relates to phrenology, a pseudo-science suggesting that features of face and head shape may reflect personality. Van Helsing admires Mina as an exception, commenting that "*young ladies*" do not always have good memory of facts.

Mina initially shows him the shorthand diary rather than her notes. Van Helsing admires her caution and laughs " *you so clever woman*". This seems an unusual time to seek to create misery, particularly when her husband may be threatened. Mina becomes ashamed of her attempt to puzzle Van Helsing. She shares the typewritten notes that she keeps in her workbasket. This is another sign of her production, the basket traditionally keeping sewing and knitting.

Van Helsing is excited and somewhat manic. Harker's diary has unlocked the secret of what has happened to Lucy. He uses the image of light breaking through and clouds rolling away to explain the moment of recognition.

Mina would seem to take on a traditional feminine role, becoming a supplicant on her knees begging Van Helsing to help her husband recover. Van Helsing praises her as one of life's "*good women*", and compares her to a light fashioned by God.

He asks her to keep an open mind for;

> "*the strange things, the extraordinary things, the other things that make one doubt if they be mad or sane*".

Mina also considers the blurring of the conscious and the unconscious in comparing the meeting to a dream. This also prepares the reader for the unusual events to follow. Mina entrusts him with a typewritten copy of Jonathan's journal.

There follows an urgent telegram sent by Van Helsing to Mina on his return to London at tea-time on the same day. He vouches Harker's journal to be true and assures Mina that her husband must have a strong brain and heart to have escaped Dracula's castle.

Mina's telegram in response is sent immediately at 6.30pm. She thanks Van Helsing for his thoughts while mourning the "*terrible things*" that exist. She fears Dracula, "*that man, that monster*", and the possibility that he has reached London.

Bram Stoker's Dracula: A Study Guide for A Level

Van Helsing occupies the space between certainty and doubt, what is known and what is unknown. He urges an open mind, no matter how strange events may seem.

Jonathan re-opens his journal

The 26th September provide an entry from Jonathan's journal, which he hoped he never had to start again. He expresses his emotions and explains how he has felt "*impotent*" and "*in the dark*" since leaving Dracula's castle. He is no longer fearful now someone believes him. He has met Van Helsing and feels he has "*cured*" him. Jonathan praises Van Helsing's eyebrows. Physiognomy, like phrenology, was mainly discredited by the later Victorian era but Van Helsing is amused and flattered. In a conversation with Harker he praises Mina as "*one of God's women*". Jonathan provides him with the legal documents relating to Dracula.

Seward also resumes his diary on the 26th September. It begins as a professional journal, as he notes that Renfield has returned to collecting flies and spiders. Arthur is with Quincey, and seems to be coping well with loss. Van Helsing has shown them the copy of the Westminster Gazette and asks Seward his opinion on the "*bloofer lady*". Seward is unsure of the relevance and notes "*I can hazard no opinion*".

Seward describes how Van Helsing seems to become frustrated with him. He credits him with intelligence and reasoning but criticises him for not accepting "*things which you cannot understand*". He urges him to use faith and imagination. Seward is asked to be open to seemingly "*new beliefs*", which though ancient" *pretend to be young, like the fine ladies of the opera*".

It can be interesting to note that although at the cutting edge of science Van Helsing often expresses conventional and somewhat misogynistic views on women. Even his praise of Mina is tempered by the fact that he finds her an exception to the rule.

Beyond belief

Van Helsing gives the example of hypnotism, which had been at the centre of recent controversy in separation from the contentious practice of mesmerism, which was believed to have been used in the mid-Victorian period to make patients act and behave against their will. He gives a lengthy overview of scientific progress in explaining mysteries, concluding with a reference to the vampire bat that Quincey Morris has already discussed. He compares an encounter with an Indian fakir with the "*walking dead*". Seward has recorded this lecture in his own diary and realises that Van Helsing is trying to educate him. This is summed up as he records Van Helsing's final statements;

"*I want you to believe...to believe in things that you cannot*".

Some minds can think of terror and also think of ways to combat this terror.

With Seward no closer to understanding the purpose of this talk, Van Helsing finally reveals that the punctures on the missing children were "*made by Miss Lucy*". Seward's reluctance to accept this marks him as a rational man of science.

Chapter 15

There is a noticeable quickening of pace in the narrative from this point. The chapter begins with a continuation of Seward's journal.

Van Helsing provides the reason for his lengthy explanation, suggesting it was the wish to break the painful truth about Lucy as gently as possible. He invites Seward to see the proof of this with his own eyes, vowing that there is "*no madman's logic this time*". Seward and Van Helsing plan to inspect child they have found, then to wait in the tomb using the key Arthur had left for safe keeping. The child appears to have been bitten by a bat, suggesting the tropical "*vampire*" species. On the way from the inn Seward is disorientated and scrambles around the graveyard looking for the tomb. The flowers and wreaths seem "*miserable and sordid*". Seward fears what they are doing is desecration, akin to stripping her in life. There is renewed horror - Seward expects the gas from a week-old corpse before Van Helsing saws the side of the lead coffin to show it is empty.

The Bloofer Lady

Seward refuses to believe Lucy is 'walking dead'. He suggests body snatchers may have stolen her corpse for medical studies. As they keep vigil at the tomb he remains angry. They eventually see a dim white figure holding a child.

The journal dates 27th September details how Van Helsing and Seward hid in the graveyard during the day and found Lucy in her coffin, with lips "*redder than before*" and teeth "*sharper than before*". Seward is determined to disprove Van Helsing's theory. There is an explicit reference to vampires and Lucy is described as "Un-dead". Stoker's draft title for the story was 'The Undead'. Seward struggles with his responses. If Lucy is already dead, why is there a dreadful fear of 'killing' her. Van Helsing suggests they need to stuff her head with garlic and drive a stake through her body. Seward notes this is a mutilation but continues to help as he expresses loathing for the undead.

Van Helsing considers how to persuade Arthur to join in the salvation of Lucy and plans to call him and Quincey Morris to the tomb. An undelivered not from the 27th September asks Seward to come to the graveyard with garlic and a crucifix. The initial plan is to stop anything leaving the tomb. He instructs Seward to read Jonathan's papers, hinting at Dracula's superhuman powers and command of animals.

Seward's diary on the 28th September highlights a fear that Van Helsing is "*unhinged*". He suggests Van Helsing may have committed some of the acts himself.

The group of men are summoned to meet Van Helsing on the 29th September. He asks them to promise to act, although he does not tell them all. Morris agrees immediately and Arthur agrees to anything that does not violate a gentleman's or Christian's code. Arthur is angered when Van Helsing mentions entering Lucy's tomb. The discussion is rife with Christian images of purgatory and hell, referring to the "*thorny paths* " and "*paths of flame*" ahead. Van Helsing tries to present his theory of the undead to Arthur who is angry at desecration but reluctantly agrees to observe and see.

Van Helsing holds the keys and as such is often the bringer of resolution and revelation. This is in contrast to Jonathan Harker, who could not escape the locked doors of the castle.

Chapter 16

Chapter 16 continues with Seward's diary. It refers to the same night in the churchyard. Van Helsing repeats his showing of the empty coffin. Morris responds by asking if she has been moved but shows a "*cool bravery*". Van Helsing's 'biscuit' used to protect is the Catholic Host used in Holy Communion and believed to be the body of Christ. Van Helsing explains he has an 'indulgence'. The use of the term is strange, as this referred to the medieval practice of praying or paying for a particular intention, but the men do not seem to question further. These men are Anglican but seem to accept the superstition and potential sacrilege in the same way that Jonathan took the crucifix.

When they observe Lucy now there is a physical change. She has become "*dark-haired*" and her sweet expression has hardened to "*adamantine, heartless cruelty, and the purity to voluptuous wantonness*". Her lips are blood stained and she snarls like a cat. Her eyes are "*full of hellfire*". There is an immediate focus on female sexuality and how it has been corrupted.

The descriptions continue to emphasise the seductive nature of the undead Lucy, who has a "*languorous, voluptuous grace*". Stoker repeats the adjective 'voluptuous' several times when presenting the female vampires, linking their state with immoral sexuality and availability. As with Harker's women in the castle, Lucy's voice seems unnatural and tinkles like glass. She does recognise her fiancé as she beckons Arthur; "*Come, my husband, come!*". Arthur seems mesmerised and under her spell. Once again Seward presents her gaze as hellfire and like a Medusa or a Greek dramatic mask. This is highlighted in the thought "*if looks could kill*". Seward expresses disgust for the "*thing*" that used to be Lucy.

When she responds like a trapped animal caught between the crucifix and the sealed tomb door, Arthur agrees to Van Helsing's 'cleansing' ritual. This follows a repeated pattern, one of a number of repetitions and re-workings in the text. The men will hide in the graveyard after a funeral.

Lucy is in her tomb and another reference to her "*voluptuous*" state would seem to mock her purity. The repeated use of this word suggests an active sexual desire.

The 'cleansing' ritual

The entry for the night of the 29th September has them gather dressed in black, with Van Helsing carrying a "*long leather*" bag, a larger version of his doctor's accessory. The bag is found to contain a set of operating knives and a round wooden stake, three feet long and several inches think. What follows is a grim parody or perversion of her wedding night.

Van Helsing explains to the group that as a *nosferatu* or undead she will be "*multiplying the evils of the world*", whereas if they can truly give her death her soul will be free to join the angels in Heaven. He persuades Arthur to set her free. Despite the men valuing their rational and secular scientific belief systems they participate in a ritual, with Van Helsing reading an exorcism from a missal while Arthur drives the stake through Lucy's heart.

The scene is described in graphic detail, with Arthur likened to Thor and praised for doing his duty. The corpse writhes in agony before they see a "*holy calm that lay like sunshine over the wasted face*". Light imagery is once again linked with goodness and purity. Now Arthur is invited to "*kiss her dead lips*".

Van Helsing and Seward then complete the task of beheading her and placing the garlic. They become aware of the natural world - the "*air was sweet, the sun shone and the birds sang*". It is as though natural order has been restored.

Van Helsing must return to Amsterdam but a plan is put in place to pursue Dracula, with all agreeing to take on the "*terrible task*".

TASK: Reading Response Chapters 8-16

What is the significance of Mina choosing not to read Jonathan's journal?

Why does Van Helsing insist on Dr. Seward's secrecy?

Why did Jonathan and Seward choose to start keeping journals again?

How does Stoker's use of language and imagery create a sense of horror in the description of Lucy's 'cleansing'?

3.4 "*Your girls that you all love are mine already*": Chapters 17-23

In this section we will;

- Consider how language and imagery convey writer's intentions in Dracula
- Evaluate the methods employed by Stoker to convey the patterns of natural speech and thought processes
- To show understanding of how Stoker's choice of form, structure and language shapes meanings.

Chapter 17

This chapter continues with Seward's diary. Mina is making her way to London while Jonathan investigates in Whitby. There is an example of embedded narrative as Seward cites a telegram sent to Van Helsing. We often learn about Van Helsing's thoughts and actions through the medium of Seward's recollections.

Van Helsing has prepared them for Mina, a "*pearl among women*". Moving forward from the death of Lucy, much of the text concerns itself with the power of sharing knowledge. Van Helsing has given Seward Jonathan's journal and Mina's diary to prepare.

On meeting, Seward describes Mina as "*a sweet-faced dainty looking girl*". His focus on her physical appearance and femininity seek to place her in the passive heroine role.

New technologies

Technology and innovation are often emphasised. Mina has taken a portable typewriter in her luggage. Mina and Seward travel by underground, sending a wire to the housekeeper. Seward does not wish to frighten her.

The narrative is taken up by Mina's journal for the 29th September. She has a curiosity about technology, and is intrigued by Seward's phonograph diary. There is humour at Seward's expense as he realises he does not know how to locate particular sections of recording.

Mina remains resourceful and pragmatic. She offers to copy his recordings on her typewriter. She notices that he has her papers and realises they need to establish trust. She suggests they take each other's journals and meet later to discuss experiences.

Mina has a moment of sentimentality as she looks forward to Seward's early cylinder recordings which will give the other half of a "*true love episode*" which ended with Lucy's rejection of him.

The interlaced narrative continues as Dr Seward's diary for the 29th September is presented. He notes that Mina re-emerges from listening to his recordings in tears. She finds his words "*cruelly true*" and offers to type his journal so others do not hear the "*anguish*" and "*heartbeat*".

Mina presents her belief in the importance of sharing records and information;

"*We need have no secrets amongst us. Working together and with absolute trust, we can surely be stronger...*".

Seward agrees this will help with the "*cruel and dreadful task*" ahead. There is a belief that when each has read and listened to the other's record of events they will know the other person better.

Mina's later journal entry on the same day notes that she and Seward share a space, sitting together to 'consume' the diaries. At points Mina is almost in a "*swoon*" when reading and Seward gives her brandy to recover. The reading is a "*transfusion*" of knowledge which exhausts them as much as the donations to Lucy had exhausted earlier in the text. Mina is industrious and aims to type all the recordings. She sends a telegram to Jonathan to brief him.

Consuming the text

The characters begin to do what the readers have done when considering the interlacing narrative. Mina uses scientific or empirical methods. She sets out to order all the information from the various sources chronologically, in order to build a case file against Dracula. She praises Seward, noting that the world "*seems full of good men*". She is driven by her work and does not sleep. The chapter mirrors Stoker's technique in assembling the narrative.

Seward's Diary for the 30th September notes his first impressions of Jonathan Harker. He judges him "*uncommonly clever...and full of energy...a man of great nerve*". He had been expecting a "*good specimen of manhood*" and is a little surprised by the businessman who arrives.

A further entry later that day notes both of the Harkers are "*hard at it*" assembling sources and "*knitting*" together a chronological record. Seward has learnt that the Count owns the property next door and realised Renfield has some link to Dracula. Seward visits Renfield who suddenly seems sane and expresses a wish to go home.

The narrative moves back to Jonathan's journal of the 29th September and charts his investigation. Harker notes the precision of Dracula's planning. In Whitby he visits Billingham's solicitors, the coastguards and Customs. He has to supply a number of working men with drinks in exchange for information.

He continues his search on the 30th September, this time in London, and after giving the station master a drink tracks down the removal men who carried Dracula's boxes. There is sarcasm as he notes these men also wish for a drink, "*the medium of the currency of the realm*". They describe the dust and decay of Carfax and inform Harker that 50 boxes were taken to London.

Mina's journal for the 30th September admires her husband's "*true grit*". A meeting is arranged with Arthur and Quincey. They have heard of Mina through Lucy. Mina tells them that she has read all the documents and has prepared everyone a copy of records so far.

Mina spends time with Arthur and notes how it may be her "*woman's nature*" that causes him to break down and weep. She takes his hand and offers to be a sister "*for Lucy's sake*". The imagery also suggests that Mina fulfils a maternal, nurturing role as Arthur "*cried like a wearied child*". Mina is aware of this as she notes there is "*something of the mother in us*". She compares Arthur's "*big sorrowing man's head*" to a "*baby that some day may lie on my bosom*".

Morris also recognises Mina's comforting role feeling she is best placed to comfort "*trouble of the heart*". Mina offers friendship to him which he accepts, kissing her hand and calling her "*little girl*".

By the end of the chapter there is a collective record. Not only are the characters better informed but they have a social bond and no secrets. Where Dracula operates through domination and deceit, the group have shown trust and honesty. This communication will help humans combat the threat presented.

> **TASK: Presentation of Character**
>
> What does Stoker suggest Mina's role is in relation to the male characters at this point in the narrative?

Chapter 18

The chapter begins with Seward's diary for the 30th September. Everyone has shared information. Mina brings tea, noting "*this old house seemed like home*", an unusual observation on an asylum. Mina shows curiosity and asks to see Renfield. Renfield 'tidies' by eating flies and spiders. Renfield addresses Mina lucidly and with courtesy. Seward is surprised by his "*own pet lunatic*". He believes this is Mina's "*rare gift of power*". Renfield occupies the border between sanity and insanity. He is trying to resist Dracula's power.

Renfield suddenly refers to trying to kill Seward. There is an odd goodbye as Renfield addresses Mina "*I pray God I may never see your sweet face again. May He bless and keep you!*" This should be read as forewarning Mina as if he were able to escape Mina could avoid Dracula.

TASK: Examination-Style Task – Presentation of Renfield

The following task is based on a task set for AQA Language and Literature Paper 1. It requires analysis of language use in an extract and other parts of the novel. In this extract, Dr Seward describes Mina Harker's first meeting with Renfield.

Explore the significance of the character of Renfield in the novel.

You should consider:

- the presentation of his character in here and at other points in the text
- the use of fantasy elements

His method of tidying was peculiar: he simply swallowed all the flies and spiders in the boxes before I could stop him. It was quite evident that he feared, or was jealous of, some interference. When he had got through his disgusting task, he said cheerfully: 'Let the lady come in,' and sat down on the edge of his bed with his head down, but with his eyelids raised so that he could see her as she entered. For a moment I thought that he might have some homicidal intent; I remembered how quiet he had been just before he attacked me in my own study, and I took care to stand where I could seize him at once if he attempted to make a spring at her. She came into the room with an easy gracefulness which would at once command the respect of any lunatic – for easiness is one of the qualities mad people most respect. She walked over to him, smiling pleasantly, and held out her hand. 'Good evening, Mr Renfield,' said she. 'You see, I know you, for Dr Seward has told me of you.' He made no immediate reply, but eyed her all over intently with a set frown on his face. This look gave way to one of wonder, which merged in doubt; then, to my intense astonishment, he said:– 'You're not the girl the doctor wanted to marry, are you? You can't be, you know, for she's dead.'

Van Helsing joins them and praises Mina's intellect, her "*man's brain...and a woman's heart*". The reader may be surprised when he then states that as a woman she can no longer be part of the pursuit. It is typical of Van Helsing's speech that he garbles idioms and uses some unusual constructions. This is used throughout the text to show he speaks English as an additional language. There is a further reading session before dinner.

Mina's journal for the 30th September suggests they are working as "*a board or committee*". Mina places herself as secretary. There follows a long record of Van Helsing's exposition on vampires. Mina aims for a flavour of his idiosyncratic speech. There is some reiteration, such as the fact Dracula has the strength of twenty men and command of weather and animals. He suggests Dracula has had a link to necromancy. He suggests that they face a life and death situation and if others become like him it will be "*a blot on the face of God's sunshine*".

Bram Stoker's Dracula: A Study Guide for A Level

All join hands as a contract. There is a business-like efficiency as they need to treat this *"as any other transaction in life"*. Van Helsing highlights the *"power of combination"* and the strength of their scientific knowledge. He considers human strengths, including the freedom to act and think both day and night and the *"self-devotion to a cause"*.

Van Helsing provides an overview of Dracula's ancestry, tracing vampires to invading races. He lists the forms Dracula has been seen in and notes that he can appear younger but needs blood.

While Dracula can see in the dark he must be invited in and lacks powers in daylight. Water can only be crossed on high and low tide and sacred items and garlic can keep him away. Ways of killing vampires include sacred bullet, beheading and use of a wild rose. The speech presents the vampire's powers but also highlights there is some hope in the face of terror.

Van Helsing outlines the plan to find Dracula and confine him to his coffin. He does digress to note that Dracula was a *voivode* or lord and in past times was the *"cleverest....bravest in 'land beyond the forest'"*, with a *"mighty brain"* and *"iron resolution"*. It may be noted these are qualities Van Helsing also possesses. Van Helsing combines personal experience with learning of folklore. The strength of their pursuit will be founded on science and knowledge.

Van Helsing suggests Dracula was a powerful lord corrupted by necromancy. There is an irony that although demonic vampire must lie in sacred earth. Van Helsing explains this opposition;

"this evil thing is rooted deep in all good, in soil barren of holy memories it cannot rest".

Quincey has left the room when shortly afterwards a pistol shot shatters the window. He rushes in to explain he shot at a bat. This is an odd interruption which leads some critics to question Quincey's status as outsider and potential threat. The planning continues to confront Dracula when weakest between noon and sunset. Mina is told she is too precious to risk and reluctantly accepts their chivalry. The men set off to investigate Carfax; Mina notes *"Manlike, they had told me to go to bed and sleep"*.

The following entry is taken from Seward's diary and is precisely dated 1st October 4.00am. Renfield has sent a message and all men go to his cell. As with Mina he seems gentlemanly and expresses a wish to leave. He worries he is *"not my own master"*. He wants to be saved from guilt but will not divulge further details. He is menacing in his reminder to Seward that he already asked him to leave.

Chapter 19

The chapter begins with Jonathan Harker's journal which records with equal precision '1st October 5.00am'. It is perhaps ominous that he begins by reassuring himself that Mina is *"strong and well"*. He recognises his wife's *"energy and*

Bram Stoker's Dracula: A Study Guide for A Level

brains and foresight" but expresses belief that her part is "*finished*". The chapter considers the importance of duty. The men feel it is their duty to fight evil. There is an irony. While it is noble to want to protect Mina from harm, their decision to exclude her and provide her with sleeping medicine leaves her vulnerable to Dracula's attack.

Harker records that Morris had felt Renfield was serious in his claims. Seward had explained that he could not release Renfield as he has some link to the Count. Van Helsing has given each man a 'cleansing' bag, with crucifix, garlic, revolver, knife, lamps and a sacred wafer. Van Helsing is equipped with skeleton keys. Harker imagines these are similar to those used to open Lucy's tomb. Van Helsing seems to hold the keys when others are locked from things.

As they explore Carfax, Harker overcomes fear of darkness and dust. They make their way to the chapel which is linked to Hell with its "*malodorous air*". The place is "*stagnant and foul*", with a "*dry miasma*" in the atmosphere. Jonathan reacts strongly to the decaying chapel, which seemed "*as though corruption had become itself corrupt*".

TASK: Exploring Gothic Elements

Consider the descriptions of Carfax and the men's actions as they proceed on their quest.

How does Stoker make use of Gothic imagery in his presentation of the setting?

How does Stoker create a sense of fear?

How do the gaps in the text contribute to the horror? You should consider clues provided regarding Mina's changing state.

The men are shocked to find only twenty-nine of the fifty boxes. Harker imagines the "*evil face*" everywhere. The place swarms with rats but Arthur's terriers will not cross the threshold to hunt. They eventually do and chase them away. The men seem content, feeling they have achieved a "*difficult and dangerous*" mission. The irony of the belief that Mina has been safe from harm is soon to be revealed.

Jonathan does not that she is "*paler than usual*" when he returns but seems typically paternalistic when he is glad she was not involved as it was "*too great a strain for a woman to bear*".

> **Miasma theory**
>
> *The booming population of London in the nineteenth century brought with it a sharp increase in contagious diseases. Methods of transmission and sources of contagions were not fully understood.*
>
> *Reformers and medical professionals still supported the "miasma theory". This proposed that disease could be airborne and transmitted through foul smells. Various governments spent time and money seeking to mask foul odours in the city of London, believing this would alleviate disease. Prominent reformers such as Edwin Chadwick outlined their support of the 'miasma theory'.*
>
> *It was felt the working class and slum dwellers had perhaps lost "The sense of smell… which generally gives certain warning of the presence of… gases noxious to the health"*
>
> *To fight disease, the city took measures to improve "drainage" and " the removal of all refuse".*
>
> *Harker's description of Dracula's Purfleet lair makes reference to a "miasma", and there are repeated descriptions of the dank and fetid atmospheres in Dracula's other properties. In this way Dracula is explicitly linked to the spread of disease and social degradation. He pollutes London and despite his noble lineage is associated with the disease-ridden slums through the stench with surrounds him. It can also be noted that in attempting to defeat the vampire, a miasma is also created. Lucy's sickroom is stuffy with the smell of garlic and this is commented on a number of times.*

He notes their work is "*a sealed book to her*". While this is celebrated it is the opposite of the openness and trust Mina herself encouraged and will ultimately place her in peril.

A later entry dated 1st October describes how he has overslept as Mina was slow to wake. He blames this on exhaustion, although cannot explain why she wakes with a look of "*blank terror*".

Seward's diary for the 1st October notes that Van Helsing was "*jolly and cheerful*" as he asked to visit Renfield. Van Helsing is as pleased as Harker that Mina is "*no more to be pained, no more to be worried*". Seward agrees Carfax is "*no place for a woman*".

Mina's Recollections

The reader is finally presented with Mina's journal, also for the 1st October. She calls herself "*a silly fool*" for complaining about exclusion. She placates herself to know that Jonathan will tell her all someday, yet feels "*strangely sad and low-spirited*".

She recalls going to bed without anxiety. She cannot remember going to sleep but has a memory of howling dogs and Renfield praying. There are visions of "*black shadows*" and a "*thin streak of white mist*". The reader is aware of some similarities to Lucy's experiences. Mina seems to have forgotten Dracula's various forms when Lucy was victimised.

Mina felt lethargic and "*weighted*" by dreams, with a sensation that the air was "*heavy, and dank, and cold*". She imagined a fog in the room. She is aware of a presence and "*lay still and endured, that was all*". Images of a "*pillar of cloud*" and the gas "*shining like a red eye*" links to Lucy's dreams and sleepwalking. Mina is aware there are similarities to Jonathan's moonlight mist and remembers a "livid white face bending over me out of the mist". She tries to rationalise as a bad dream, and strives hard to sleep naturally. There is perhaps a moral ambiguity and sense of guilt in Mina's troubled sleep due to her being a married woman. As with Renfield's inversion of John the Baptist, Mina's pillar of cloud recalls the Bible telling of God leading the Hebrew slaves to freedom yet here it is a manifestation of Dracula, who will seek to oppress.

The entry for the 2nd October is noted as 10.00pm. Renfield asked to see Mina and wished her God's blessing before crying. Mina thinks of the men's welfare and seeks to cheer them on their return. She asks Seward for a sleeping draught but soon realises she may want to stay awake.

Chapter 20

This provides a continuation of Jonathan Harker's journal from the 1st October. He has tracked down the moving company. Jonathan gives a snapshot of the London poor. Contact Thomas Snelling is already drunk on beer but directs Harker to Joseph Smollett. He does keep a notebook detailing where Dracula's boxes have gone. He recalls worker Sam Bloxam mentioning a dusty house in Purfleet, but warns that he may also be drunk at this time of day. Smollett offers to post details back to Jonathan.

Harker returns to find Mina "*a little too pale*" and sleepy. He plans to send her back to Exeter. Reading Smollett's information he initially struggles with the poor spelling but follows clues to the newly developed cold storage building. Throughout the novel, Stoker makes passing reference to new technologies, here including a building with early refrigeration techniques. Harker has to make use of more "*coin of the realm*" - offers of alcohol - to find information about Dracula's boxes. He is surprised to hear some have been sent to Piccadilly, then a more affluent area of London. One of the workmen recalls a strong, thin "*old feller*" assisting with the move.

Tracking Dracula

Without keys or door numbers, Harker uses an educated guess to work out that the dilapidated house in Piccadilly is most likely Dracula's. He uses deduction to find the estate agent and pretends to be employed by Lord Arthur Goldaming in order to gain information.

On getting home he finds Mina is now "*tired and pale*" and as he sends her to bed she seems "*more affectionate with me than ever*". The reader may be realising the nature of her illness in the similarities to Lucy's behaviour. It may be that Harker's satisfaction at investigating the boxes of earth has distracted him from observing the significance of the changes in his wife.

Seward's diary for the 1st October is then presented. Arthur, Quincey and Jonathan are out investigating, while Van Helsing maintains a focus on records to gain an "*accurate knowledge of all details*". Seward is puzzled by Renfield and his mood changes. Renfield is clear in not wanting souls - "*Life is all I want*". He believes himself to walk with God. Seward interprets Renfield's "*dogged silence*" and finds him "*sulky*". He can admit that he often visits Renfield as a way to pass the time. Meanwhile, Seward somewhat taunts Renfield, telling him he cannot have life without souls. He views Renfield as a child. This links with Victorian criminology and later discussion of Dracula's "*child brain*". Renfield will not use the word 'drink', causing Seward to ask what he means. The reader may be frustrated that Seward cannot make the links to other events. He has established there may be some link between Renfield and Dracula but fails to see Mina is endangered. Seward treats Renfield as a scientific experiment, using empirical methods and listing behaviours. He is no closer to solving the puzzle but fears "*some new scheme of terror afoot!*". Van Helsing joins Seward on a later inspection of Renfield deeming him " *a curious case indeed*". Once again the boundaries between sanity and insanity are found to be slight.

The narrative presents a letter from Mitchel, Sons and Candy to Lord Arthur Goldaming, also dated 1st October. It provides information on the house at 347 Piccadilly. The men know it to be Dracula and he seems to be mocking with the false name he has used. Count de Ville has clear suggestions of hellish intentions.

Money once again is seen as a vehicle for corruption, as part of the reason the agents did not research references was the fact he paid a large amount of cash.

Seward's diary of the 2nd October detail the meeting of the men after Mina has gone to sleep. The guards have reported Renfield as praying loudly. The plan is to sterilize the earth in Dracula's boxes. Van Helsing has been at the British Museum investigating ancient medicines. There has been a shift in beliefs as Seward now discusses "witch and demon curses" in normal conversation. He still doubts his sanity;

" *I sometimes think we must be all mad and that we shall wake to sanity in strait waistcoats*".

He later hopes this will be the "*beginning of the end*". Renfield interrupts with a "wild yell". They find him "*all covered in blood*". There is urgency, with a switch to present tense.

Chapter 21

The journal entries are not in true chronological order. This is perhaps as a result of excluding Mina from the investigation and serves to highlight the various points of view. With the model of trust and collective information failing, Dracula now dominates.

Seward's diary of the 2nd October once again emphasises the need to keep records with "*exactness...as well as I can remember*".
Renfield has been found with a bloody face, broken back and limbs and paralysis to the face. His injuries cannot be explained as happening at once. He is described as "breathing stetorously", in a similar, animalistic style to Lucy. There was no attendant to witness the injury. Van Helsing want to be alone with Renfield as he regains consciousness. He plans to use trepanning to treat the skull fracture.

Mina's Transformation

Arthur and Quincy now appear. All seem to dread what Renfield may say. Renfield tells them of his "*terrible dream*". He recalls a mist, red mouth and white teeth. He combines images of moths, flies then rats, as he sees flames, mist, and then a red cloud the "*colour of blood*". He called out "*Come in, Lord and Master!*"

He saw gleaming red eyes and a vision of Mina in her room, pale "*like tea after the teapot has been watered*". He reveals Dracula "*had been taking the life out of her*". Renfield tried to grasp the mist, but there is a red cloud and a noise like thunder before he was flung down. This is Renfield's dying testimony.

The men grab their hunting kits and despite fears of disturbing a lady's room, gather to shove the door of Mina's room open. Seward recalls "*What I saw appalled me*". In the bright moonlight they see Jonathan, with his "*face flushed and breathing heavily as if in a stupor*". Mina is kneeling and there is a tall, thin man, dressed in black with a scar on his forehead. Mina's hands are held back and she is blood-smeared and seems to be drinking his blood against her will, like a

"*child forcing a kitten's nose into a saucer of milk to compel it to drink*".

Meanwhile the man's "*eyes flamed red with devilish passion*".

Stoker may have been inspired by the story of St Catherine of Siena drinking Christ's wounds

Stoker repeats descriptions, as the *"white aquiline nose"* clearly identifies this man as Dracula. He springs at them like an animal. The men wave a crucifix, from which he recoils and turns into vapour. Mina then screams as Quincey runs in pursuit of the vampire and Harker wakes in *"wild amazement"*. Mina holds her husband and when presented with a crucifix rests on him, putting blood on his shirt. She wails that she is now *"unclean, unclean!"* and quickly understands her changed state. She knows she has become Harker's *"worst enemy"* and must not kiss or touch him.

Harker begs Seward to tell him what happened. Seward repeats elements of the story. There is an observation that Mina's hair has been stroked for comfort, which contradicts the earlier detail of the Count restraining her hands while forcing her to his chest.

The group then discover that Dracula has burnt the manuscripts and thrown the wax recordings on the fire. Seward reminds the others there are copies in the safe. Renfield is now dead, and Quincey returns to say that Dracula has gone westwards.

Van Helsing asks Mina to recount her version of events. She remembers taking a sleeping draught but then fighting sleep and bad dreams of death, vampires and blood. She implores Harker to be strong and help her. Eventually she slept but woke to a white mist in the room. She cannot recall if she has shared her recent diary which mentioned the mist a few days earlier. Mina could not wake Jonathan as a tall man in black with fiery eyes appeared. She remembers being paralysed with fear as the man threatens to dash Jonathan's brains out. The man attacks her throat as *"a little refreshment"*. She recalls not wanting to stop him, even as she is disgusted by the *"reeking lips"*.

The man is dismissive and vengeful as he punishing her for trying to *"play your brains against mine"*. Mina is made an active participant as he attempts to dominate and control her, his revenge for her defying one *"who commanded nation"*. Language use recalls the bible and the marriage ceremony. He tells her she is now his *"flesh of my flesh, blood of my blood, kin of my kin, my bountiful wine-press"*. He uses her and tells her she will now come to his call. He forces her to drink his blood.

Mina is aware she is now *"in worse than mortal peril"*. She wipes her lips *"to cleanse them from pollution"*. Her fear of pollution echoes the patriarchal Victorian view of sexual and moral corruption discussed in the Contexts sections of the guide.

It is noted that in the short time since discovery Jonathan's face has gone grey and he now has *"whitening hair"*.

Chapter 22

Jonathan's journal of the 3rd October explains his need to note his thoughts *"or go mad"*. He feels this is a test of faith for him and Mina. Renfield has been eventually found with his neck broken. Seward had planned to note the attendant's evidence and death by misadventure to avoid an inquest.

Following events, Jonathan feels Mina now needs to be *"in full confidence"* of developments. His wife announces that if she harms any she loves she *"shall die!"* This is not hyperbole - she would rather commit suicide if no-one could perform euthanasia, which Van Helsing has offered. Van Helsing is however firm - *"you must not die"*. Mina must try to outlive Dracula to avoid becoming one of the Undead. There is a Christian message as she aims to fight with her *"living soul"*.

Van Helsing notes that she is "*so good and brave*". He assures the group that Dracula was not fully aware of their plans. Despite the focus on death there is a call to live and fulfil duty.

While Dracula is in mortal form during daylight they plan to sterilize his boxes of earth, trapping him in a body which can die. The aim is to persuade a Piccadilly locksmith that they need re-entry into the house. Arthur is told his carriage with the Goldalming crest will attract too much attention. Seward, Van Helsing and Harker will go to Piccadilly while the other men investigate boxes in other parts of London. Harker can scrutinise Dracula's legal papers to ascertain his plans.

Van Helsing's humour seems inappropriate when he says the city is safe from Dracula's attack as "*last night he banqueted heavily*". This is unnecessarily cruel to Mina and he does apologise immediately for the "*stupid old lips of mine and this stupid old head*". This does show that he is fallible and human, and also that he holds the gender prejudices of the time is suspecting a degree of complicity in the attack.

"Unclean!"

Mina's room has been prepared to keep Dracula out. Van Helsing places the holy Host on her head, which makes an immediate burn and scar. Mina is hysterical, once again claiming she is polluted "*Unclean! Unclean!*" and now has "*mask of shame*". Van Helsing does not contradict but does say God will help her on Day of Judgement. The men see themselves as righteous agents of good.

Jonathan is troubled and offers to join his wife as a vampire, proof that

"*the holiest love was the recruiting sergeant for their ghastly ranks*".

The plan is revised. Quincey and Arthur will walk to Piccadilly and persuade a locksmith to let them into the house. This continues the motif of keys and access. Jonathan should not take part in this part of the plan to avoid losing place with Law Society. The house "*smells so vilely*". The blood in the washbasin marks the space as unclean. Eight boxes of earth found mean one is still missing.

Chapter 23

Seward's diary provides an insight into Jonathan's changed character. He has been "*overwhelmed, in a misery*". Despite his relative youth overnight he has become a "*drawn, haggard old man*". This is a physical manifestation of the impact of evil. He does retain energy in his pursuit of Dracula which Seward feels powers him "*like a living flame*".

Van Helsing once again digresses to outline how impressive Count Dracula was in his lifetime;

"*He has a mighty brain, a learning beyond compare, and a heart that knew no fear and no remorse*".

He could have been a great man but has chosen the occult and has fallen from grace. Now he feels the undead Dracula is "*only a child*", with a "child-brain". He is experimenting and testing his powers.

Mina can communicate with Dracula at sunrise. The narrative is interrupted with a brief dispatch from Mina, noting Dracula's movements from Carfax. The use of telegrams help to build the suspense, creating a sense of urgency as the reader joins the group on the pursuit.

Harker is initially driven by vengeance, desiring "*to wipe out this brute from the face of creation. I would sell my soul to do it!*". This places doubt on his character. Given religious beliefs at the time, his love for Mina is clouding his judgement. His response to Dracula's evil actions threatens his own soul.

Van Helsing reminds him of God's justice, and likens their plan to a crusade or mission, stating "*we are all devoted to this cause*". There is still an emphasis on deduction and scientific method. Van Helsing notes the tide times and works out when Dracula has crossed river. The group are asked to be ready as a key turns in the lock. This ratchets up the suspense.

Confronting Dracula

The Count makes a cautious entry, "*panther-like in the movement*". He remains animalistic, responding to them with a "*snarl*" and look of "*lion-like disdain*".

Harker is uncharacteristically violent. He cuts at Dracula with a kukri knife and while he misses, bank notes and gold pour out of the Count's coat. Dracula bleeds money as well as blood.

Seward challenges Dracula with the crucifix and wafer, resulting in a raging response, as Dracula throws himself at the window, grabbing at his gold before tumbling out. He is not repentant, comparing the line of men to "sheep in a butcher's". He mocks them, reminding them that as an immortal he has centuries to act. He threatens Victorian womanhood as he boasts:

"*Your girls that you all love are mine already*".

This threat is not sexual, but based in a desire for power, as he threatens to attack men as well as women:

"*you and others shall yet be mine, my creatures, to do my bidding...*"

Some critics have read this speech, one of the few moments where Dracula is given a voice in the narrative, as evidence of the threat of reverse imperialism. Dracula as outsider will conquer London culturally in the daylight, acquiring property and learning customs, while he will take his victims at night, building an army of undead.

Van Helsing notes fear. He sends the younger men as "*hunters of the wild beast*". He takes the money and the title deeds, and burns the rest of the papers. Despite her own problems, Mina shows empathy and pity for her "*husband's grey head*". Again Stoker utilises symbolic use of white and red. Mina is 'snowy white' with fear, yet blushes red at the devotion shown to her by others. Harker remains angry and desires to send Dracula's soul "*to burning hell*".

Harker's journal is marked as the 3-4th October as he write close to midnight. He is "*yearning for sleep*" yet remains anxious that one box is missing. Mina is "all perfection". Jonathan is ashamed by her ability to show pity for the Count and his solitude. She urges they show mercy and pity his soul when they do confront him. She believes Dracula to be the "*saddest case of all*". The couple hear something in the corridor outside their room. They are reassured that Quincy Morris is standing guard, as he is one of the "*good brave men*".

Jonathan writes on wakening early on the 4th October. Mina insists on sending for Van Helsing so he can hypnotise her before dawn and perhaps learn of Dracula's plan. Again the sense of time adds to urgency. In her trance she hears "*lapping of water*", suggesting Dracula is on a ship. Van Helsing's response is full or digressions but suggests they track money used for escape, comparing search to a fox hunt. Mina initially asks why they cannot just forget Dracula now he has left. She is told that if he escapes she will die and remain cursed.

TASK: Thematic Concerns

'The conflict between reason and emotion is characteristically Gothic.' Consider how far you agree with this statement, using support from the text.

Bram Stoker's Dracula: A Study Guide for A Level

3.5 "*We shall follow him, and we shall not flinch...*": Chapters 24-27

In this section we will;

- *Consider how language and imagery convey writer's intentions in Dracula*
- *Evaluate the methods employed by Stoker to convey the patterns of natural speech and thought processes*
- *To show understanding of how Stoker's choice of form, structure and language shapes meanings.*

Chapter 24

This section is recorded as being spoken directly by Van Helsing, but as forming part of Seward's phonograph diary recordings. The Count would seem to be returning home and while Van Helsing is glad they have driven him back from London despite centuries of planning. Van Helsing knows they have to conquer Dracula fully. He is confident Dracula "*is finite*" while as a group they are "*all more strong together*". Van Helsing serves as a foil to Dracula. He has described the Count's patience, strength and learning, yet also possesses these qualities. Both men are evoked with language of dominance and mastery.

Harker's journal for the 4th October has a further entry. Jonathan has read the transcript of Van Helsing's message. Mina is comforted by this and seems stronger. Her own experiences seem "*a long forgotten dream*" although the scar is a harsh reminder and a proof of contamination. The couple would seem to embrace the Victorian work ethos, as they fear idleness. They pick through the diaries for further clues. Mina sees them as "*instruments of ultimate good*". There is a fear to speak of the future.

Mina's journal of the 5th October is provided. It is recorded as 5.00pm. She has written up the minutes of the meeting and recorded an attendance list. This provides a formal, business register, and validates the pursuit of Dracula.

In pursuit of Dracula

Arthur Goldaming uses his influence and experience to suggest Lloyd's list as a way of checking ships which may have left for the Black Sea. They find the Czarina Catherine is going to Varna. When interviewing men at Doolittle's Wharf those they meet are loud and swear frequently. "*Blood*" and "*bloom*" are euphemisms for curse words. Van Helsing's English seems more stilted in this recount. He does describe the Count's action at the wharf. On a day where the mist became a fog, the Captain is angry at his demands but Dracula did not seem offended. He was not seen boarding at high tide.

Van Helsing provides a long and detailed account of the ship setting sail. The plan is now to defeat Dracula while in his box between sunrise and sunset. They have details of the acting agent at Varna. They use Mina's hypnotised state to verify that Dracula is still at sea. Van Helsing would seem to lose temper but recognised *"at least some of that personal dominance which made him so long a master amongst men"*.

This strength can be seen in Van Helsing himself, although he uses this mastery for the common good.

Transylvania is regarded as having *"strangeness of the geologic and chemical world"*. There is a suggestion that there are occult forces, but there are also scientific explanations for the caverns and waters with strange property.

A Christian crusade

Having recognised Dracula's resilience, Van Helsing nevertheless believes that a Christian world *"will not be given over to monsters"*. He makes a direct comparison to the Christian crusaders, likening their group to the *"old knights of the Cross"*. They will also travel East towards the sun. Some may doubt the motivations of those who would seek the mastery of men, which could be seen as a more fearsome sign of a monster than bloodsucking.

Mina counters that Dracula may now be cautious, and may wait like a tiger. Van Helsing replies that once a tiger tastes flesh, it will hunt again. While claiming Dracula had a *"child-brain"* he still demonstrated patience and planning in moving to London. There is admiration for the learning and what he achieved *"alone, all alone!"*.

Mina begins to relax until she sees the mark on her forehead. There is evidence of traditional beliefs as she deems herself *"still unclean"*.

Seward's diary of the 5th October echoes earlier entries. He remembers the horror of seeing Mina's forehead. Seward and Van Helsing aim to privately discuss *"the vampire's baptism of blood"*. They fear that Mina is changing and that some characteristics of the vampire are emerging. Van Helsing suggests they do not share plans with her. Mina has taken to excluding herself.

They try to predict the timing of the ship's crossing. They aim to use trains and technology to allow them to outpace the Count. Quincey suggests arming themselves with Winchester guns to deal with wolves, which prompts an anecdote about adventures with Arthur.

Jonathan's journal for the 5th October highlights his conflicting loyalties. He must conceal information from her to keep them safe. There is silence before Mina asks him to promise not to tell her. Mina herself seems cheerful, with the others becoming *"infected...with her gaiety"*. She is compared to a child in her sleep.

On the 6th October Mina insists she must go with them. She is honest is stating that she may get to trick Jonathan, but she explains she can help while hypnotized. She also conducts research into superstitions and suggests they could use wild rose to keep Dracula in his box. Morris vows to *"destroy the monster"*. He shows no fear of death. Van Helsing tells all to get their affairs in order, so all may be "*ready for what may come*". Harker makes use of his diary as Mina "must not hear them now". There is a shared belief in the group being "*instruments of ultimate good*".

Chapter 25

The analysis of Dracula had noted the selfishness of his "*child-brain*". Van Helsing would argue that a "*man brain*" is made in God's image, with a capacity to reason. All of the group will grow in the service of God.

We move to Seward's diary for the 11th October. Jonathan asks Seward to keep records as he is no longer able to. Just before sunset Mina's old self re-appears. Seward notes the difference between "absolute freedom" and "*internal struggle*". Mina remains a loyal wife. She faces the truth, "there is a poison in my blood". She now vows that she must not commit suicide. This is not through fear; rather, a belief that it is God's will that she confronts Dracula, even if eternal rest is risked. She would damn herself to Hell if it meant defeating his evil. Mina is not a gentle martyr. She argues that it is easy for "*brave men*" to give lives. She asks for a promise that they will kill her if the time comes that she is "*dead in the flesh*" and once undead, they must stake and behead her. She wants to die in grace.

Quincey is first to agree, telling her he will not flinch. Van Helsing, Arthur and Seward then agree, with some reluctance. Jonathan's love is leading him to despair rather than hope. He seems unwilling to kill Mina should it be required. This relates to a wider debate on euthanasia. Victorians held views sympathetic to traditional beliefs, where dying is seen as a test of courage and virtue. Jonathan cannot bear it but she asks him to think about times in history when men have killed wives to preserve their honour and would prefer it to be by his hand.

Mina is relieved when they agree but fears her links with evil. She asks they perform the Christian burial service for her now. Seward records that he is emotional. The break in his voice is represented in his text; " *I cannot go on...words...and v-voices...f-fail me!*" They take some comfort from praying together.

There are further gaps in the record, with the next entry being from Jonathan Harker's journal, having now reached Varna. There is some record of the journey, including the novelty of being on the Orient Express. Jonathan is too preoccupied to note any incidents on the journey. He is pleased that Mina now looks well and has some colour, although she sleeps for much of the time. He perhaps missed the links to how Lucy behaved just before death. Van Helsing now hypnotises Mina twice a day. She "*yields at once*", again providing a link to Lucy's sedated transfusions.

Arthur received a series of telegrams stating the ship was not reported. He goes to the consulate to get permission to board the ship. It seems bribery and money was used to delay docking. As with earlier there is a link between money and power, "*Judge Moneybag will settle this case*".

The plan falters

The 16th October entry notes that Mina now has limited information. On the 17th October Arthur invents a story that the box has stolen goods. The group reason that if they stake the Count in his box he will turn to dirt and no-one will be tried for murder. If arrested, they hope the journals and records will save them "*from the rope*".

The next entry for the 24th October has no report of the ship, promptly followed by a telegram for Arthur on the same day claiming ship has been seen in the Dardanelles.

Seward's Diary of the 25th October notes his preference for recording voice on phonograph. The men were excited by the telegram although Mina has become lethargic. In a private conversation with Van Helsing, he agrees that if her teeth become sharper "*euthanasia*" may be required. Seward acknowledges this neutral sounding word hides the action.

By noon on the 25th there is still no sign of the ship. Harker sharpens his knife, ready for vengeance. Van Helsing and Seward remained worried about Mina.

26th October shows still no sign of the ship, which they suspect is delayed by fog. When this is still the case on the 27th October the group concede it is "*most strange*". Arthur receives a telegram on the 28th of October to say it has been seen in Galatz, many miles away.

Seward's diary of the 28th October suggests they had been expecting this but hoped it was not the case. Harker now has a hopeless and bitter smile. Mina is practical as ever and informs them that the next train leaves at 6.30am. There is a flurry of activity as they attempt to arrange onward travel.

Mina is energetic and keen to write. Van Helsing suggests that the Count has "*cut her off*". While they have lost intelligence, they hope they can outwit his "*child brain*". They do not want Mina to despair, with Van Helsing hiding his hysterics. Van Helsing takes a long time to explain what he has read in Jonathan's journal. He expands on his theory about Dracula's "*child brain*" and Mina is allowed to contribute to the discussion.

Chapter 26

The group split into pairs; Seward and Morris, Harker and Lord Goldaming, Mina and Van Helsing. The interlacing narrative and overlapping dates carry the text towards a rapid conclusion. Elements of the narrative are not fully rationalised, as why Van Helsing would take Mina towards the castle and other vampires.

Even when separated, there is clear evidence of empathy with others and mutual co-operation. This underscores the unity of their quest in opposition to the tyrannical domination of Dracula.

Seward's diary of the 29th October notes that the trains have helped them to regain control. Van Helsing now questions Mina. She mimes lifting a weight with hands and Van Helsing knows Dracula has left the box and is approaching land. It is taking longer to hypnotise Mina. Fate would seem to conspire against them as they are three hours late and will not intercept Dracula.

A change of plan

The entry for 7.00am on the 30th October describes the approach to Galatz. Mina is edgy while the rest of the group are "*on fire with anxiety and eagerness*".

The narrative is taken up through Mina's journal for the 30th October. Quincey takes Mina to a hotel while Arthur visits the Vice Consul. Mina still strives to piece together a schedule in her weakened state.

Jonathan's journal for the 30th October details how he went with Seward and Van Helsing to the agents. They board the ship and meet Captain Donelson. He recalls the Romanian crew making two finger gestures to ward off the evil eye as the box was loaded. There was a dense fog during the journey. He directs them to the removals agent Immanuel Hedesheim, who removed Dracula's box from the ship.

In his portrayal of Hedesheim, Stoker relies somewhat on derogatory Victorian stereotypes of Jewish merchants. As with the London estate agent, Hedesheim notes his employer as a Mr de Ville. Gold changed hand and a man called Skinsky took the box. He was later found with his throat torn out.

Mina Harker's entry on the evening of the 30th suggests the pursuit has picked up pace. She keeps her diary on a travel typewriter, another example of modern technology supporting the pursuit of evil. She describes Jonathan as a weak victim.

Her journal is interposed by a memorandum, a logical list of what she surmises about the Count's journey. She compares the pros and cons of travelling by road, rail or water. Dracula's ship had travelled unnaturally fast. She now deduces travel would be most likely on a particular river. The men thank her for her diligence and work, before meeting for a 'Council of War'. Arthur will travel by steam launch while Quincey will travel by horse. Seward would go with Quincey on a 'hunt' with Winchester guns, while Harker will go on the steam boat. Still Mina hesitates to write 'Vampire'. Van Helsing agrees that Jonathan should be allowed to kill Dracula. Van Helsing and Mina will re-trace Jonathan's earlier journey and make their way to Dracula's castle. The metaphor of the hunt continues as Dracula seen as "*an old fox*".

Mina praises the men as being:

"*so earnest, and so true, and so brave!*" yet notes the reality of "*the wonderful power of money!*"

Arthur and Quincey have funded this part of the mission. Mina shows precision with the train timetable. She is armed as the men but cannot hold the blessed bread due to her scar. Snow flurries and wolves recall the horror of Jonathan's early trip to the castle. She steels herself to have *"Courage, Mina!"*.

Paired Pursuit

Jonathan Harker's journal for the 30th October is written by the furnace as Arthur loads the fuel. The narrative is interlaced as we move between the groups in pursuit of Dracula. They take comfort in their faith in God and hope to outrun Dracula with the speed of the steam boat.

He notes that Seward and Morris will track the right bank and treat it like a *"wild adventure"*. The entry leading into the 1st November notes boats that they pass, one flying a Romanian flag. The men tell them there is a boat travelling at double speed. Harker oversleeps in the 2nd November before taking over at the helm. He tries to imagine the progress of the other pairs.

This dovetails into Seward's diary of the 2nd adventure which notes *"no news"*. The snow is coming but he still treats as an adventure.

Mina Harker's journal on the 31st October notes that Van Helsing has failed to hypnotise her. They have to purchase a horse and carriage for the final 70 miles of the journey. Mina can acknowledge that this is a *"lovely"* country and imagines sharing the journey with Jonathan. She tries to remain positive during dinner but is aware her future is *"in hands of God"*. She thinks about Jonathan and assumes her own death, hoping *"Jonathan may know that I loved him"*.

Chapter 27

Mina records in her journal of the 1st November that the horses seem to work with them and travel at speed. Van Helsing persuades some farmers to exchange horses. Mina appreciates scenery *"full of beauties of all imaginable kinds"*. When a woman sees Mina's scar she makes the evil eye gesture. Garlic is put in the food. Van Helsing seems to be tireless but urges Mina to rest. Mina's response to hypnotism has stalled. She observes Van Helsing to be *"very tired and old and grey"* but admires how *"his mouth is set as firmly as a conqueror's"*. Even when asleep he seems *"intense with resolution"*.

The themes of life and death are constantly in play. Mina now has the liminal existence of the vampire, on one had looking healthy and on the other entering the limbo of the un-dead.

Mina has her own strength, taking turns in driving horses. She notices that the air becomes heavy and oppressive. Her entry for the night of 2nd November places them near the Borgo Pass. She invokes God frequently now, and fears she is *"unclean to His eyes"*.

There follow a memo from Van Helsing. Dated the 4th November, it is addressed to John Seward. Mina is now sleeping by the fireside. She sleeps constantly and has lost her appetite. She no longer keeps her journal. He fears the evening when she is as "*sweet and bright as ever*". Van Helsing evokes a higher power as he asks "*God's will be done*". Van Helsing's contribution now offers to fill the gaps in Mina's journal.

On the Borgo Pass Mina seemed to intuitively know the route to the castle. She explains it is due to Jonathan's journal. The roads are less clearly marked. This serves a symbolic function as their future is not clear. Mina has been sleeping heavily and cannot be hypnotised. She has a ravenous appetite, becoming like an animal. Van Helsing notes that she is has a higher colour and fears she is becoming a full vampire.

The final conflict

On the morning of the 5th November Van Helsing recognises the importance of recording events; "*Let me be accurate in everything...you may at first think that I, Van Helsing, am mad*". It continues the theme of questioning sanity common to all journals. As the castle comes into sight both the sun and moon reflect in the snow, creating a "*great twilight*". This is a liminal time between day and night. Van Helsing sets up a fire and a ring of blessed wafer. The sacred symbols are evoked yet used in a pagan ritual in the construction of this 'magic ring'. This juxtaposition is not necessarily disparate as the circle protects as the presence of Christ will do.

He tests Mina by calling her to the fire. If she cannot cross it at night, it will protect him from other vampires. The horses are disturbed and the snow and mist takes the form of the vampire women. They begin to circle as Mina urges him not to leave his holy circle.

Mina is strong, and laughs at the women to show that she does not fear them. Van Helsing is in danger and twice suggests an attraction in the use of the word "*kissed*". Mina is horrified as they call her "*sister*". They depart. There is fear as the horses are found dead.

The narrative moves backwards to Jonathan's journal of the 4th November. He describes an accident with the steam launch and wishes they were with Morris and Seward.

A brief extract from Seward's diary notes the wolves, snow falling and the Szgeny people gathering.

Van Helsing's memorandum of the 5th November describes how he leaves her within the holy circle. Using Jonathan's diary as a guide, he explores the castle. He suggests the old chapel is full of "*sulphurous fume*", conjuring images of Hell. He seems lacking in empathy when he leaves Mina outside, suggesting that if the wolves attack it would be God's will. He suggests death would provide freedom from Dracula's curse - the "*maw of the wolf*" is better than the "*grave of the vampire*".

He searches for the resting place of the women, once again noting their "*voluptuous beauty*". Van Helsing differs to Jonathan in that he can recognise the women are attractive, but can also distance himself in musing that men may be hypnotised and paralysed by the Undead women. He recognises his own paralysis and desire for sleep, yielding to a "*sweet fascination*".

His thoughts are disrupted by a wail from Mina which prompts him to action. He appreciates the beauty of the fair vampire as "*so exquisitely voluptuous*", but does not allow this to impede his "*wild work*". He places a wafer in Dracula's tomb before staking all three female vampires. He notes his own violence as "*butcher work*", but celebrates that souls have been won as a result of "*my butchery*". The destruction of the female vampires recalls Lucy's staking as they crumble to dust.

On reaching Mina, she howls in pain. She awaits her husband - it is ambiguous whether she is referring to Harker or Dracula. This is one of many examples of doubling in the novel. Mina's pale appearance is a sign that she is fighting the transformation.

In Mina's journal of the 6th November, she notes they are travelling towards Jonathan and can now see the castle in "*all its grandeur*". The constant howling of the wolves is both wild and uncanny. They must shelter in a hollow in the rocks. They make use of field glasses, similar to modern binoculars, to see men approaching with a wagon with a box on it.

There is now a race against sunset, when Dracula's power will be restored. Van Helsing once again makes a Holy Circle. He fears they are too late. At once, they see Morris and Seward approach. There are more horses, carrying Arthur and Jonathan. The group have converged. Van Helsing shouts "*in glee like a schoolboy*".

There is snow yet the sun is shining bright. Wolves are gathering. There is a snowstorm and an hour of light remaining. This becomes a chase, as Jonathan calls "*Halt!*". The men draw guns while Dracula's men draw weapons. Even Mina feels a "*wild, surging desire to act*". Jonathan and Quincey Morris are singular in purpose. Dracula's box is flung to the ground and they cut at him. Morris cuts through with a bowie knife, fighting on even when stabbed in the side. Jonathan is armed with his kukri knife. The men work together to open the box. There seems to be no further resistance. The Count is lying "*deathly pale*" and is compared to a "*waxen images*". His eyes remain tinged with evil intent, as they "*glared with the terrible vindictive look*". As the sun sets, they note his "*look of hate turned to triumph*". Quincey plunges his bowie knife in Dracula's heart while Jonathan sweeps his knife across his throat.

The tone changes as "*like a miracle*" Dracula's body "*crumbled to dust*". Mina is capable of some empathy and expresses relief that Dracula's face finally had a "*look of peace*". They notice the castle standing stark against the sky, with the broken battlements prominent. Dracula's men flee and the wolves retreat. Attention turns to Quincey Morris, who is dying. The group unite around him. He is not despondent. His final words confirm he is "*happy to have been of service*". His last utterance calls to God and notes that Mina's forehead is clear of the scar.

The group agree that Quincey "*died a gallant gentleman*". Morris is a key emblem of the theme of self-sacrifice. He has served until death.

Jonathan's End-Note

The novel ends with a note or postscript from Jonathan from seven years after the events described. In some ways this balances the opening statement.

He vows that he and Mina now have happiness and it has been "*well worth the pain we endured*". They have a son, born on Quincey's death date. Both Harkers believe his spirit lives on in their son. They have named their child after all the members of the group in recognition of their bond. Jonathan explains that they have visited Transylvania that year. Both Arthur and Seward are now happily married. As they sit with Van Helsing on a visit, Jonathan reflects that when evaluating the various journals and memos there is "*hardly one authentic document*". He argues that they could hardly ask others to accept "*as proof of so wild a story*". The final image the reader is left with is a family group, with the child sitting on Van Helsing's knee. Van Helsing counters Jonathan's view. He claims they will "*want no proofs*" and the child will grow to know how "*brave and gallant*" his mother can be.

The final reflection suggests that "*later on he will understand how some men so loved her, that they did dare much for her sake*". The ultimate aim seems to be the protection of Victorian womanhood.

The note is signed Jonathan Harker, suggesting that his voice has framed the narrative throughout. As a lawyer, he may be seen to give legitimacy to the "*wild*" story.

TASK: Language and Imagery: Religion in Dracula

There is a concentration of Christian language and religious imagery in the closing chapters of the novel, as the group strive to defeat Dracula before he reaches the safety of his castle.

To what extent does Stoker's use of language and imagery present a narrative of good against evil in the final section of the text?

Part Four: Contexts of Reception

Part Four:
Contexts of Reception

4.1 Contemporary Reception
4.2 Critical Contexts and Approaches: Genre-Based and Structuralist Approaches
4.3 Critical Contexts and Approaches: Psychoanalytical and Gendered Readings
4.4 Critical Contexts and Approaches: Historicist and Post-Colonial Readings

4.1 Critical Reception

In this section we will;
- *Demonstrate understanding of the significance and influence of the contexts in which literary texts are written and received*
- *Explore connections across literary texts and contexts*
- *To show understanding of how Stoker's choice of form, structure and language shapes meanings.*

Contexts of Reception: Critical Responses and Linking Texts

As well as appreciating the **historical contexts** of the novel presented in **Part One: Contexts of Production**, you will be expected to develop an understanding of how readers have received the novel. This can be in a range of contexts. It can be useful to consider how readers at the time reacted to the narrative and its presentation of childhood. Where this information is hard to come by, it can be illuminating to consider how the writer was viewed at the time of writing and this forms part of the reading activity later in this section.

Another form of reception is **critical reception**. This involves exploration of academic responses to the text, usually written by researchers with a literary background. This is good preparation for higher level undergraduate study and can also serve to provide new perspectives on the text which you may not have considered.

Last but by no means least, you must learn to value your own **response as a reader**. Barthes argued for the 'death of the author'. A text will only mean what the reader wants it to mean. The examination will encourage you to present your own interpretations of the presentation of particular themes linked to the idea of childhood.

Contexts of Reception: Contemporary Reviews

When the book was published in 1897, contemporary critics were less likely to comment on the theme of sexuality and were more critical of the text for the reliance on sensationalism and "*mawkish sentimentality*". The Daily Mail found it "*a weird and ghostly tale*" (*Daily Mail*, 1st June 1897).

Stoker's employer, renowned actor and Lyceum theatre owner Henry Irving seemed less than supportive when he announced the dramatic reading of Dracula was "*Dreadful!*" It should be noted that this was a rushed public reading in the theatre to secure Stoker's copyright of the novel.

Fellow writer Sir Arthur Conan Doyle, most famous for his Sherlock Holmes stories, wrote an enthusiastic letter to Stoker praising *Dracula*:

Letter to Bram Stoker from Arthur Conan Doyle, August 20, 1897

My dear Bram Stoker,

I am sure that you will not think it an impertinence if I write to tell you how very much I have enjoyed reading Dracula. I think it is the very best story of diablerie which I have read for many years. It is really wonderful how with so much exciting interest over so long a book there is never an anticlimax. It holds you from the very start and grows more and more engrossing until it is quite painfully vivid. The old Professor is most excellent and so are the two girls. I congratulate you with all my heart for having written so fine a book.

With all kindest remembrances to Mrs Bram Stoker & yourself.

Yours very truly,

A Conan Doyle

Doyle reflects the Victorian love of sensation and horror in his joy at the *'diablerie'* in the novel. He compliments the pace of the narrative and Stoker's creation of suspense. Van Helsing is singled out as an engaging character. The labelling of Lucy and Mina as *'girls'* may irk the modern reader.

Victorian reviews would often focus on content and narrative, as in the review presented in *The Times*, which provided caution to certain readers:

Dracula cannot be described as a domestic novel, nor its annals as those of a quiet life. The circumstances described are from the first peculiar...The only chance of stopping it was to kill the Count before any of his victims died,...and how it is managed forms the subject of the story, of which nobody can complain that it is deficient in dramatic situations. We would not, however, recommend it to nervous persons for evening reading.

The Times, 23rd August, 1897

Some contemporary reviewers were unconvinced by the juxtaposition of supernatural and new technologies and felt the story should have been set in a distant historical past. A review in *The Spectator* on the 31st July 1897, described the mix as '*incongruous*' and ultimately off-putting:

> Mr. Bram Stoker gives us the impression — we may be doing him an injustice — of having deliberately laid himself out in Dracula to eclipse all previous efforts in the domain of the horrible, —...for all these, and a great many more thrilling details, we must refer our readers to the pages of Mr. Stoker's clever but cadaverous romance. Its strength lies in the invention of incident, for the sentimental element is decidedly mawkish. Mr. Stoker has shown considerable ability in the use that he has made of all the available traditions of vampirology, but we think his story would have been all the more effective if he had chosen an earlier period. The up-to-dateness of the book — the phonograph diaries, typewriters, and so on—hardly fits in with the mediæval methods which ultimately secure the victory for Count Dracula's foes.
>
> *Spectator*, 31st July, 1897

More scathing was a length review in the arts magazine *Athenaeum*, which suggests Stoker 'almost succeeds' in writing a gripping horror story:

> *Athenaeum* 26th June, 1897
>
> The strengthening of a bygone faith in the fantastic and magical view of things in lieu of the purely material is a feature of the hour... Mr. Stoker is a purveyor of so many strange wares that 'Dracula' reads like a determined effort to go, as it were, "one better" than others in the same field....Mr. Stoker's way of presenting the matter, and still more the matter itself, are of too direct and uncompromising a kind. They lack the essential note of awful remoteness and at the same time subtle affinity that separates while it links our humanity with the unknown beings and possibilities hovering on the confines of the known world. 'Dracula' is highly sensational, but it is wanting in the constructive art as well as in the higher literary sense. It reads at times like a mere series of grotesquely incredible events; but there are better moments that show more power, though even these are never productive of the tremor such subjects evoke under the hand of a master. An immense amount of energy, a certain degree of imaginative faculty, and many ingenious and gruesome details are there. At times Mr. Stoker almost succeeds in creating the sense of possibility in impossibility; at others he merely commands an array of crude statements of incredible actions.

There would seem to be a split between high and low art.

Reviews in regional newspapers in Derby and Bristol aimed at general readers wrote about *Dracula* in mainly positive terms:

> Mr. Bram Stoker's "Dracula" will suit readers who delight in literary nightmares...To write a book of this kind properly requires a very strong pen indeed; and it may truthfully be said that the author tells this impossible variant upon the old tradition in a way which conveys the idea of reality, and produces all those peculiar sensations which are to be expected from the "shocker" novel. "Dracula" is cleverly constructed, skillfully and strongly told, has a strong hold upon the imagination, and will hold its own with the few really powerful stories of its kind which have lived in literary history.
>
> Derby Mercury 23rd June 1897

> To those who are fond of the ghastly and the gruesome, "Dracula" will be welcome reading. The story is cleverly constructed and brilliantly told, and we do not think we can add further praise to the manner in which Mr. Bram Stoker sets forth the mysterious and the awful...
>
> The Bristol Times and Mirror, 8th June, 1897

Theatre review publication *The Stage* presented a mixed response. They had praise for the opening chapters but were wary of the various complications in the plot:

> The Stage, 17th June, 1897
>
> Mr. Bram Stoker has already made his mark as a writer of romances, but in his latest book, Dracula,...he has done more ambitious work... In surrounding his gruesome and fantastically supernatural root idea with a framework plainly matter-of-fact and purely of 19th Century structure, Mr. Stoker has, we think, gone too far in the introduction of complicated details. As the book also contains much about hypnotism medically employed, semi-medieval philosophy, and applications of the latest information concerning the workings of the abnormal brain, it must be conned very carefully indeed if the reader wishes to grasp all the threads in the author's elaborately constructed argument...
>
> The opening chapters of Mr. Stoker's brilliant tour de force (are)... more artistically done than the somewhat involved and disjointed conclusion...Mr. Stoker has a keen eye for the picturesque and the appropriate in his choice of epithets and in his word-painting, and many passages of his story are indeed remarkably written...brings in...the stabbing of women recently notorious in London.

> The author has, perhaps, knocked the nail too often upon the head in his constant allusions to the exact periods of the day during which the Un Dead may arise from their mouldy earth-filled coffins, but yet all who are attracted by the supernatural in literature will find fascination enough in Mr Stoker's Dracula.

The *Daily Mail* reviewer was a fan. Avoiding spoilers, he describes how he read novel in one sitting, which resulted in nightmares:

> It is said of Mrs. Radcliffe that when writing her now almost forgotten romances she shut herself up in absolute seclusion, and fed upon raw beef, in order to give her work the desired atmosphere of gloom, tragedy and terror. If one had no assurance to the contrary one might well suppose that a similar method and regimen had been adopted by Mr. Bram Stoker while writing his new novel Dracula. In seeking for a parallel to this weird, powerful, and horrorful story our mind reverts to such tales as The Mysteries of Udolpho, Frankenstein, Wuthering Heights, ... But Dracula is even more appalling in its gloomy fascination than any one of these...The recollections of this weird and ghostly tale will doubtless haunt us for some time to come. It would be unfair to the author to divulge the plot. We therefore restrict ourselves to the statement that the eerie chapters are written and strung together with very considerable art and cunning, and also with unmistakable literary power. Tribute must also be paid to the rich imagination of which Mr. Bram Stoker here gives liberal evidence. Persons of small courage and weak nerves should confine their reading of these gruesome pages strictly to the hours between dawn and sunset.
>
> The *Daily Mail*, 1st June, 1897

Bram Stoker's Dracula: A Study Guide for A Level

TASK: Exploring Contemporary Reviews

The review below was published in the *Manchester Guardian* in 1897.

- Which elements of Stoker's writing style have been praised?
- What do you understand by the rating of the book as *"more often grotesque than terrible"*? (Bear in mind the Victorian use of 'terrible' suggests terror).
- What are the similarities and differences between this and a modern review?

A writer who attempts in the nineteenth century to rehabilitate the ancient legends of the were-wolf and the vampire has set himself a formidable task. Most of the delightful old supersitions of the past have an unhappy way of appearing limp and sickly in the glare of a later day, and in such a story as *Dracula*, by Bram Stoker (Archibald Constable and Co., 8vo, pp. 390, 6s.), the reader must reluctantly acknowledge that the region for horrors has shifted its ground. Man is no longer in dread of the monstrous and the unnatural, and although Mr. Stoker has tackled his gruesome subject with enthusiasm, the effect is more often grotesque than terrible. The Transylvanian site of Castle Dracula is skilfully chosen, and the picturesque region is well described. Count Dracula himself has been in his day a medieval noble, who, by reason of his "vampire" qualities, is unable to die properly, but from century to century resuscitates his life of the "Un-Dead," as the author terms it, by nightly draughts of blood from the throats of living victims, with the appalling consequence that those once so bitten must become vampires in their turn. The plot is too complicated for reproduction, but it says no little for the author's powers that in spite of its absurdities the reader can follow the story with interest to the end. It is, however, an artistic mistake to fill a whole volume with horrors. A touch of the mysterious, the terrible, or the supernatural is infinitely more effective and credible.

4.2 Genre-Based and Structuralist Approaches

In this section we will;
- *Demonstrate understanding of the significance and influence of the contexts in which literary texts are written and received*
- *Explore connections across literary texts and contexts*
- *To show understanding of how Stoker's choice of form, structure and language shapes meanings.*

Early Critical Reception

Some early readers were repulsed and somewhat surprised at the content of the novel, as Stoker himself had previously expressed horror with 'lewd subjects'. We need only recall his comment to William Gladstone in 1897 that

> "There is nothing base in this book" (Letters). He later writes in the journal *The Nineteenth Century* "the only emotions which in the long run harm are those arising from sex impulses" (Stoker, 1908).

It is important to note that the novel *Dracula* never explicitly discusses the sexual nature of interactions with vampires. While convinced that the novel deals with psychological and sexual issues, Richardson (1959) believed that Stoker may have been genuinely unaware of the erotic content of the text. Belford in her biography of Stoker argued that the writer would be well aware of the potential to shock and excite his audience due to his long experience working in theatre.

Stoker was drafting Dracula around the same time as the emergence of Freud's theories and the birth of psychology, and while he may have not encountered Freud in the original German, he could well have been familiar with debates regarding gender and sexuality due to the intellectual interests of his social circle. Those who challenge this notion point out that Freud discusses the 'uncanny' and makes reference to vampire myths without mentioning Dracula as late as 1912, although it could be countered that although Freud was either unaware or unconcerned with Stoker's popular text, Stoker may well have been conversant with early psychology. There is some supporting evidence in the text as Mina and Van Helsing reference Charcot in a discussion, an early mentor and guide for Freud.

Bram Stoker's Dracula: A Study Guide for A Level

Critical Reception: Academic Sources

Let us now turn our attention to literary criticism. A-Level and IB Literature students may already familiar with this type of text from work on other units. When working independently with texts, as you will for this unit, you may encounter critical readings intended for undergraduate and postgraduate readers. They can be quite daunting but with a bit of exposure to these types of texts, you will gain confidence and should be able to draw on the information presented in them to present original ideas about your literature texts. Throughout this section, the details of the sources of further critical discussion are provided and these can provide you with extended learning opportunities.

Twentieth century critics have admired the foregrounding of the new Victorian technologies such as Seward's phonograph recordings and Mina's typewriter in contrast to the medieval methods ultimately employed to restore Lucy's soul and conquer Dracula. It may be argued that the attempt to contain and overcome this supernatural force with rational and mechanical records was the secret of the texts success in a Victorian society which embraced empiricism and the scientific method.

Other readers have found it fruitful to consider the genre of the text and how it may have been received by readers at the turn of the century. A number draw attention to its status as a fantasy.

Structuralist Approaches

The text presents a series of first-person narratives combining journals, recordings, letters and other documents. The sustained horror and confusion presented in Harker's journal is soon apparent in the communications of others. As with the earlier Gothic text Frankenstein, the embedded layers of narrative enhance the feeling of confusion and the claim for authenticity.

The text can be seen as a series of structural oppositions. From the outset Dracula and Harker can be seen as a conflict between old and new. David Punter (1980) suggests that where Dracula represents aristocracy and feudal lineage, the others represent family; Dracula functions in the wild night, the others are secure in the day; Dracula and his vampires experience bitter passions while most characters aim for reason; Dracula is the physical and erotic, while other relationships are shown as idealised love or repression of urges. For Punter, Dracula represents *"passion which never dies, the endless desire of the unconscious for gratification, which has to be repressed in order to maintain stable ideology"*.

Punter explains that the Gothic world is not only more inexplicable than the realist world, not merely fantastic but an alternative reality, *"a different kind of truth"*. If the mind is regulated by needs of interaction with the world then some material must be repressed. The text hints at this murky psychology.

For Punter, the Gothic

"takes us on a tour through the labyrinthine corridors of repression, gives us glimpses of the skeleton of dead desires and makes them move again" (Punter, 1980).

Punter draws attention to the role of reanimation of legends, ballads and folk tales. Vampire legends are centuries old but from early nineteenth century become aligned with modern anxieties.

Stoker builds on the vampiric tradition and the characteristics of literary vampires. The women in Stoker's take on animalistic qualities and as in Le Fanu's *Carmilla*, the victims have an ambivalent response which mixes excitement and disgust. He also links physical journeys to psychological elements.

Dracula and the 'Uncanny'

Ernest Jones (1929), a disciple of Freud, considered the role of vampires and vampire myths in relation to taboos and sexual fantasy. Jones suggests the vampire embodies "most kinds of sexual perversions" and " *a return to the sexual anxieties of the child*" . It should be noted that explicit discussion of sex was not accepted in texts at Stoker's time. "*In writing a fantasy he was able to encode ideas, fears and desires*" and present in a form acceptable to a reading public.

In Harker's encounter with the women of the castle there is confusion of the familiar and the unfamiliar. Harker recognises their differences yet feels as though he recognises the fair-haired woman. This reinforces the sense of the uncanny.

The 'Uncanny'

Fantasy is both a literary genre and a term from Freudian psychology. While still in its infancy as the text was begin written it is clear that the text draws on the concept of the uncanny, and this was identified by a number of contemporary readers.

Andrew Bennett and Nicholas Royle explain the uncanny as relating "specifically with a disturbance of the familiar". This can be seen in a number of ways in the opening chapters, as when the domestic chores in the castle seem to be completed without human agency. The Count's movement down the walls, his lack of reflection and lying in a box of earth all disrupt. The text presents " the vampire as an uncanny being, who occupies a strange, transgressive state that defies the boundaries of life and death, yet who at the same time has something about him familiar"(208). This is drawn from Freud's essay Das Unheimliche (The uncanny or 'unhomely') and links to ideas of repression.

While the model of the uncanny emerged after the text, there was a general interest in the unconscious at the fin-de-siècle, with curiosity regarding both the paranormal and the emerging field of psychology. Stoker was clearly aware of Charcot, whom he had referenced in the novel and while a direct access to Freud's work cannot be traced, he did have close friends in 'Physical Research', including Frederic Myers, who had given a lecture of Freud.

In Freud's discussion he noted that the word for 'uncanny' was also the word for 'unhomely'. The second set of meanings for heimlich or homely equates to something concealed or hidden from others. Grimm's dictionary of 1877 also suggests that belonging to the home is also those things which can be concealed from strangers. The translation perhaps loses some of this nuance and ambiguity but it remains that home can be a place of secrets as well as a place of comfort and security. This ambiguity underpins Freud's reading of relationships - the uncanny is not new or alien but something familiar which is alienated or changed through repression.

Dracula as a Gothic text

Some readers feel Stoker was influenced by earlier Gothic texts such as Mary Shelley's *Frankenstein*. Both stories involve fears surrounding monstrosity and creation. Chris Baldick sees Dracula as a variant of Frankenstein's monster. In the earlier text the monster was created by a human and as such was an allegory for the dangers of excessive knowledge and endeavour within humans, while in Dracula the fear is outside. While Frankenstein subverts creation, Dracula subverts death and mortality.

Eva K Sedgwick also feels *Dracula* embodies a number of the features of Gothic writing, namely:

- Through setting; often narratives were set in Catholic European countries
- Oppressive landscape with castles, and ruins.
- Stock characters such as the sensitive heroine, the impetuous lover and tyrannical older man
- Tropes and features such as religious institutions, characters in a trance or deathlike state, subterranean spaces, burials and 'doubling'
- Unnatural echoes or silences, or difficulties in communication.

> **TASK: Harker's time at the castle**
>
> Can you find evidence of each of the Gothic features listed in the opening four chapters?
>
> Some of these elements are discussed below.

The opening has elements of the realist novel in its depiction of the travelling businessman. Harker borrows heavily from the genre of travelogue as he recounts his experiences in his journal. Bistritz is presented as foreign yet 'civilised'. This is in sharp contrast to his journey further into the Carpathian Mountains. There is an immediate threat from the wilderness and nature intimidates Harker with the baying wolves, jagged mountain peaks and 'ghost-like clouds'.

As Harker baulks at the 'vast ruined castle', he is placed in the position of the conventional heroine travelling towards doom. Dracula fulfils the role of the aged tyrant with the mesmerising gaze. Harker is passive and submissive as the women enact a sexual assault on him. At this point in the narrative, his fiancée Mina Murray is the shadowy figure of the lover who is far away.

Harker seems to remain in a dream state as he explores the vault and seems in a trance when the women appear. Later in the text Lucy will enter a deathlike state before her actual demise in her recurrent sleepwalking. Mina will communicate with Dracula under hypnosis.

The narrative is disrupted by breaks in Harker's journal. Harker has entered the story as a symbol of modernity and the burgeoning legal profession but is powerless entering this 'domain of ancient feudalism'.

This is enacted through language as Dracula's impassioned speech highlights that his house equates with his lineage. A psychological reading would feel the castle reflects the owner. Both provide a juxtaposition of the decayed yet imposing. Both hide secrets. Here there are echoes of Bluebeard's wives, or more recent texts such as *Jane Eyre*, with the house containing terror. As with the more traditional heroine, Harker is forbidden from certain spaces and in violating this puts himself in moral and physical danger.

Gothic 'doubling' is evident in the Count's use of Harker's clothes to implicate him in the disappearance of the local child. It cites both men as 'other' in relation to the close-knit and religious villagers. Harker eventually has to mimic the Count in a desperate attempt to flee the castle, making his way down the wall he had seen Dracula, down previously. Likewise, both men write letters.

Chapter 5 sees an abrupt shift to the realist mode, with an exchange of letters between Mina Murray and her friend, Lucy Westenra. Mina had a degree of independence as a Victorian schoolmistress with a control and competence with the new technologies of typewriting and short hand as forms of communication. At this point in the narrative the women would seem to be conventional heroines of nineteenth century plots with their interchanges on love and marriage. It is noteworthy that the text has moved from the solitary act of keeping a journal or diary to the social medium of letters.

Through the text, Gothic and realist elements are intertwined. Mina and Harker use shorthand as a code, foreshadowing the ways in which new technologies and approaches will support the battle against the supernatural. Conversely, the ruins of Whitby Abbey and the fascination with tales of ghosts and imprisonment draw on the Gothic elements fore-grounded in the opening chapters set in Dracula's castle. In the novel, the deserted residence at Carfax, the asylum, Highgate cemetery and the shadowy house at Piccadilly transport the Gothic to a more familiar setting for the readers.

The enemy in the Urban Gothic is both evil and unnatural. In this way Dracula can be seen as the "conservative fantastic". The modern reader should ask what threat did Dracula represent in 1897 and how would culture and society protect itself from this threat.

Victorian Gothic

Both *The Turn of the Screw* and *Dracula* define a sense of the modern for the Victorian reader. *Dracula* can be considered as supernatural or part of an occult tradition that uses supernatural horror as a reminder of the sacred in the everyday.

Dracula can be seen as a double of the priest-like Van Helsing. The reader is presented the texts as a compilation and does not doubt the veracity of the calms as Harker doubts his own records at the end of the text. The transcription is a 'transfusion' of the experience.

Dracula is a typical Gothic fiction:

> "The Gothic Tradition culminates in Stoker's remarkable power to convey a sense of presence; a sense of power, meaning, understanding that explains and naturalised the horror of the past - the terror of temporality - by discovering the sacred within (or at least behind) the fullness of moving time, the Profane.
> **Ronald Schleifer in *The Trap of the Imagination***

The central metaphor of the grave creates a space. Even as they move across continents they are defined by closings-in and confinements. The mystery is to find what already is there. The past co-exists with the modern world and threatens to engulf it. There is more to know than can ever be known and the characters are waking into darkness.

The world of the book is presided over by Dracula's presence. The text explicitly draws attention to writing. As a transcript of speech which will outlast the speaker, writing itself may be considered immortal. Within the transcription is the sense of characters being locked into a dream. The importance of movement and rest is stressed in the novel - the displaced corpses must rest, later the groups must move to hunt Dracula.

The plot of the novel involves the gathering of letters and getting the record straight. The primacy of imagination over reality and the elevated status of reactions are typical Gothic features. The text is marked by a 'stopping short', marked by repetitions and anticipations.

The narrative gap displayed at moments such as the discovery of Mina and Dracula recalls attempts to interpret old paintings. The recurrent action of the text is to write and organise, to make sense of the world. The action is often interrupted as characters attempt to represent experience and record it.

Dracula's presence is created through the narration. The search for meaning is constantly constrained by time. Characters strive to stay awake, even in the face of horror. The text asserts life against death. Dracula may subvert healthy sexual relations and thwart Lucy's marriage, but the novel concludes with a blessing of the Harkers' marriage with a child.

The child Quincey Harker is the novel's final text – he is the literal full stop of the endnote. In not speaking all of the child's names, Jonathan is perhaps reminding the reader that Dracula's blood flows through him as well.

Throughout the text characters inhabit borders between waking and sleeping, questioning reality and dreams, sanity and insanity. The characters are seeking meaning and social communication. This search for sexual, social and cultural origins literally haunts *Dracula* and the Gothic tradition.

Dracula as a 'fantastic' text: Todorov and the Fantastic

Tzvetan Todorov (1973) rejects psychoanalytical readings of literature. He believes that fantasy is based on conflict between the creation of a familiar world and events that cannot be explained by laws governing society or nature. The reader will finally decide that the event is either an illusion of the senses or that the event has taken place. This then supports belief in the marvellous or the uncanny. If marvellous, this acknowledges the element of supernatural, while uncanny involves the effect of making strange produced by the distorted or distorting mind of the protagonist.

For Todorov, the fantastic is only part of the work. The ambiguity is resolved as reader accepts as marvellous or uncanny. One exception is suggested in *The Turn of the Screw* by Henry James which sustains ambiguity relating to the state of mind of the governess at the very end of the narrative.

Further, to be regarded as fantastic the text must comply with at least two of the following three conditions:

- The fictional world is one of living people, causing reader to hesitate between natural and supernatural explanations.
- Hesitations must be experienced by characters and evident in themes.
- The reader would reject allegorical or poetical interpretations.

Now let us apply the model to *Dracula*. When Van Helsing proposes a supernatural explanation - vampires - there is a hesitation shown in the discussion with Seward. This reluctance to accept the supernatural continues until the encounter with Lucy in Highgate cemetery. Narrators constantly question their sanity. It would then seem that the text is in the realms of the fantastic or marvellous.

However, the novel does make use of multiple viewpoints, with an emphasis on note-making, and an insistence on comparing points of view to negate misinterpretation. These aspects undermine the ability to read the text as an example of Todorov's uncanny, referenced in Part One.

The novel concludes with an abrupt twist. Harker re-examines the papers seven years later and is struck by the lack of concrete evidence. He looks at a pile of typewritten accounts. The final note throws the acceptance of the supernatural into uncertainty. This hesitation would suggest a fantastic text.

The fantastic and the mimetic

Rosemary Jackson (1981) maintains that Todorov's approach has limited relevance when reading *Dracula*. She argues that by refusing to acknowledge any form of psychological reading, Todorov is ignoring ideologies present in fantastic literature.

She counters that fantasy is deeply concerned with the unconscious and the subconscious. As the world of the unconscious is often resistant to being represented in language this can be located in the gaps, silences, unspoken understanding and difficulty in naming threats.

Jackson(1981) noted that fantasy has been used as a broad term to describe any literature *"which does not give priority to realistic representation... presenting realms 'other' than the human"*.
Additionally, fantasy has

"an obdurate refusal of prevailing definitions of the 'real' or 'possible', a refusal amounting at times to violent opposition"
(Jackson, 1981)

Dracula begins in the realm of the vampire. Bloodsucking can be found in nature but here these once human creatures return from the dead, transgressing the boundaries between life and death, neither *"fully alive nor decently dead"*.

Fantasy was popular as a genre at the time of the novel. Dracula could be grouped with texts such as *The Strange Case of Dr Jekyll and Mr Hyde (*1886), and *The Picture of Dorian Grey* (1896). These texts share a fear of the monstrous or monstrosity.

Jackson argues that a psychoanalytical reading provides a frame for understanding unconscious thought, Novels can explore the tensions between individual desire and social 'norms' through the 'code' of fantasy. She suggests Todorov's model can be extended if the politics of the form are considered. Rather than focus on structure and formal elements the reader should consider the ideological concerns presented in both form and content.

Jackson also evaluates Todorov's use of the term 'uncanny'. She replaces Todorov's terms of 'marvellous', 'fantastic' and 'uncanny' with the term 'mimetic'. Jackson explains that the marvellous is distanced in to the past while the mimetic claims to imitate external reality. The text should be designed to elicit an emotional response. The mimetic has an authoritative and knowing narrator; *"the fantastic conflates elements of both the marvellous and the mimetic (or realist)... in the fantastic mode, the narrator shares the reader's uncertainty, constantly questioning and wondering what is 'real' "*.

Fantastic fiction relies on the real to define itself. Van Helsing urges Seward to look beyond possible explanations for Lucy's illness. If realism is considered a style relating to the 'bourgeois' or middle class, fantastic fiction highlights fears of the community relating to the unknown.

> **TASK: Applying Critical Frameworks**
>
> To what extent are the fears expressed in the statement below presented in the novel?
>
> ***"The process of cultural fragmentation that characterized the fin de siècle threw the norms of the Victorian age into crisis; empires were threatened, feminism was on the march, and the first socialist parties were formed"***
>
> *Cultural Politics at the Fin de Siècle* Sally Ledger and Scott McCracken
>
> You should consider:
> - Evidence of Todorov's 'fantastic' and Jackson's 'mimetic' in the text.
> - References to imperialism, gender and class.

4.3 Psychoanalytical and Gendered Readings

In this section we will;
- *Demonstrate understanding of the significance and influence of the contexts in which literary texts are written and received*
- *Explore connections across literary texts and contexts*
- *To show understanding of how Stoker's choice of form, structure and language shapes meanings.*

Psychoanalytical approaches

In the mid-twentieth century a link was made between fear of vampirism and social taboos regarding sex and death. Building on Freud's earlier discussion of the 'uncanny', the fear of the corruption of the familiar, which referenced vampire myths in anthropology, a number of critical responses to Stoker's novel sought to apply psychoanalytical approaches.

A key example is Maurice Richardson's reading in 1959, which felt the story was *"quite a blatant demonstration of the Oedipal complex"*. This reading suggests Dracula is the authoritative father-figure, an evil and powerful father who gathers women and sons to him.

Later readings would explore the focus on perversions of sexuality and motherhood, and while still identifying these using psychoanalytical frameworks, now sought to place these readings in the context of Victorian expectations of gender and family. Judith Weissman notes much of the text concerns male, patriarchal figures trying to control and purify women who express unconventional views, whether it be Lucy's flirtatious desire to marry three men or Mina's desire to master new technologies and exercise her "man's brain". Furthermore, she argues society fears the release of female sexuality that Dracula's infection seems to provide.

While critical responses in the last thirty years have provided a diverse range of readings and approaches, the psychoanalytical and psychosexual model still prove popular.

In a detailed biography of Bram Stoker in 1996, Barbara Belford identified elements of the novel as presenting a *"sexual lexicon of Victorian taboos...seduction, rape, gang rape, group sex, necrophilia, paedophilia, incest, adultery, oral sex, menstruation, venereal disease and voyeurism"*.

Writing an overview of responses to the novel, Dracula and Victorian Gothic academic Elizabeth Miller notes that the psychosexual readings of the text demonstrate as much about the society of reception as they do about Stoker's intentions. She suggests that the readings from the past thirty years which explore heterosexual and homosexual desires are a reflection of identity politics.

Readers are reminded by Robert Mighall that the staking of Lucy - often read as a violent attack on women by the dominant male patriarchy - may just be an enactment of traditional superstition regarding the slaying of vampires. In addition, the account of Lucy's 'cleansing' is provided by John Seward, her rejected suitor who admits his obsession with her earlier in the text. Alternatively, reading in a Christian framework, as is provided in the novel, this is an exorcism, albeit a violent one.

Miller notes that twentieth century critics have foisted an erotic reading on a character who is described as unattractive, with thin and cruel features and bushy eyebrows. Stoker's Dracula is a "*foul thing*", an embodiment of evil in a text filled with Christian and biblical allusions. We must take care as modern readers not to superimpose readings without secure textual support.

TASK: Evaluating Critical Interpretations: Sometimes a stake is just a stake....

There is little doubt that much of the growing appeal of Dracula throughout the twentieth century was due to the text's potential for yielding up a variety of sexual readings. This has been accompanied by an increasing tendency to identify with the vampire as the "sexually liberated" Other, an erotic force which creates undue anxiety for the repressive society which it invades. Consequently, the Victorians become the villains while the vampires promise the sexual liberation that Victorian England supposedly denied. But in the flush of excitement to validate the novel, to give it relevance in a postmodern world, one can too easily fall victim to distortion or even the creation of information to support a theory. That is where, in the view of this writer, we should pull back. For sometimes a wooden stake is just that—a wooden stake.

From **Coitus Interruptus: Sex, Bram Stoker, and *Dracula*** Elizabeth Miller

Full text at https://www.erudit.org/fr/revues/ron/2006-n44-ron1433/014002ar/

Take one of the psychoanalytical and gendered readings in this section and attempt to argue against this.

You should consider:
- Alternative interpretations of textual examples provided in the reading
- Alternative explanations for characterisation or Stoker's use of language.

Dracula: Gendered Readings

Phyllis A Roth (1977) in her essay 'Suddenly Sexual Women in Bram Stoker's *Dracula*' notes how Dracula could be seen as a father-figure. Van Helsing is the 'good' make role model while Dracula is seen as lacking. Similarly Lucy and Mina are seen as having maternal aspects -Lucy's in an abomination as she feeds from a child held at her chest in an inversion of a nursing image, while Mina nurtures and cares for the men, eventually becoming a mother to Quincey Harker in the conclusion of the novel.

Roth also argues that Dracula acts out the repressed fantasy of others, and sets out to destroy Lucy and Mina. Looking at the narrative structure, Roth feels that the victimisation of Lucy and then Mina presents " *the same story told twice with different outcomes*" (Roth, 1977).

Lucy would seem the more ambiguous character from a moral standpoint, presented as more desirable, sexualised and therefore more threatening. Mina may seem less of a threat yet still 'devours' Dracula. Roth reads Harker's recognition of the fair-haired vampire as a link to the 'archetypal mother'. Applying psychoanalytical models she suggests that Dracula is a fantasy of incest and matricide, although notes that actual families are either incomplete or limited.

The text's resolution relies on a reaffirmation of bourgeois values, as Mina and Jonathan's marriage produces a child. The bond of males has been replaced with the family unit and the threat has been contained. There is the complication that Quincey Harker is in fact of mixed blood, including the vampire blood which Mina has consumed, which in turn has had transfusions from the men via Lucy. If blood pollution is read as an analogy for fears about external threats, Quincey may actually prove that it is already too late, as the future generation carries the contagion.

Jonathan Harker: The threat to manliness

Gender is under intense scrutiny throughout the novel. Historically and socially, there was a challenge to Patmore's idealised 'Angel in the House' in the burgeoning Suffragette movement and the threat of the free-thinking 'New Woman'. Oscar Wilde's trial and conviction in 1895 made homosexual relationships the source for national scandal and the depiction of Wilde as a predatory older man fed anxiety and was seen as a threat to masculinity. Elaine Showalter has referred to the end of the nineteenth century as a period of sexual anarchy. While fears of gender are not fully articulated in Dracula there is a sense that attempts to control fear and conquer vampires are also attempts to re-establish gender boundaries.

Stoker leaves the narrative in the hands of those who will be seen as taking a lead in the future, mainly Seward and Harker. There is still a way of reading the text as harking back to earlier imperialist adventure stories. Pedlar (2001) notes the novel can be read as "*a tale of male courage and comradeship, of fighting and resourcefulness"*. Seward and Harker in particular *"reveal apprehensions and fears that show how unstable are the boundaries of self-definition"*.

It is argued that throughout the novel, Harker's masculinity is threatened in a number of ways:

- He is powerless against a tyrannical old management
- He is emasculated by the female vampires
- He remains passive and faints

When he realises the full horror of what the women plan to do to the child in the sack, he loses consciousness. Later he writes his journal and notes that he is at a table where a lady may have composed a love letter. His journal had begun as an aide-memoire of his travels, and then later was used as a rational and objective way of recording facts. After his encounter with the female vampires, he uses it as an attempt to reclaim sanity - *"I turn to my diary for repose. The habit of entering accurately must help to soothe me"*. Harker then loses his place as narrator until after Lucy's death. On his return in Chapter 14, it is Mina who has shown his journal to Van Helsing.

Experiences need to be verified by a third party. This connects to links between writing and masculinity. Once Harker feels he is believed, he regains confidence in his manhood and can take an active role as narrator.

Harker's masculinity is once again called into question in Chapter 21. Seward is asked by Harker to describe what was encountered when Dracula was discovered with Mina. Seward's description would seem to dwell on Harker's position and the relative poses of Mina and Dracula in the discovered tableaux. The imagery comparing Mina at Dracula's chest to a kitten forced to drink milk not only subverts the traditional maternal image of feeding but also suggests infidelity. Seward does not elaborate on Harker lying alongside in a sleep-like state with troubled breathing, perhaps to protect his fragile sense of masculinity.

Phillip Martin (1988) has considered the differences in Seward's accounts and the potential confusion arising relating to the references to hands, which could not simultaneously be restraining wrists, holding neck and stroking hair. Mina's account would corroborate Seward's initial description, and Martin suggests later discrepancy reflects his embarrassment on encountering what seems to be a sacrilege of the Harkers' marriage bed.

Pedlar posits that the hand stroking hair would be the hypnotised Harker as Dracula forces Mina to ingest blood. This would conflate the two male figures and indicate Dracula has usurped Harker's marital role. Seward's blending in his accounts would support this.

Mina Harker: Vampirism, Consumption and Production

The scene is described for a third time in Chapter 21 in Mina's account. Seward was unable to comment on her feelings. Mina also gives the perspective of the victim, who would only see the eyes emerging from the mist. She has previously recognised passivity, as having "*lay still and endured*" during Dracula's attack in Chapter 19. This is not a longing or sexual fascination - it suggests bewilderment at her own lack of reaction

"*...strangely enough, I did not want to hinder him*".

The unfinished sentence where she notes she had to swallow or suffocate enables the reader to feel her revulsion. Dracula has parodied the marriage service in claiming her as "*flesh of my flesh*". He has imposed a sexual reading on the encounter, assuming the conjugal role as he claims Mina as his "*companion and helper*". Dracula seeks to displace Harker and has now created a link between himself and Mina.

It seems a supreme irony that as the character who was able to exploit new technologies of communication, Mina would now become the mysterious and channel of communication between the hunters and Dracula. Having made use of modern media such as shorthand and typewriting Mina is now the medium, both as the channel which tracks Dracula and in the psychic sense as she carries messages in a trance.

Mina as Producer

In consuming Dracula's fluid, Mina also takes what has been absorbed from other blood donors. Lucy has been his victim, and she in turn absorbed blood from Holmwood, Seward, Van Helsing and Morris. Mina becomes a blood bank before making blood her own, through her son. That it is not entirely her own is evident in Jonathan Harker's postscript when he suggests their son Quincey has been a product of the group.

Some would argue that this is evidence of Dracula's contamination continuing to the next generation while a more positive reading links Mina's production as a mother with her role as editor of the various transcripts and records. She consumes or collates the materials and records produced by the other characters and types in an ordered document which is then used to study and defeat the vampire.

Mina's baby is the only child in the text seen in the context of a loving family. The vampire women seem pacified by children which the reader then believes they devour. Lucy is also seen to prey on children when confronted.

At the end of the novel, Mina is idealised and has fulfilled her 'proper' role as wife and mother, becoming an 'Angel Of the House'. Where other female characters have transgressed the maternal role and flouted decorum. The vampire women are seen as exploiting male weakness, the language used to describe them casts them as 'whores' in opposition to Mina's role as Virgin.

This reading suggests an implied critique of the monster in the midst of Victorian society, the 'New Woman'. The New Woman, like the decadent male epitomised by Oscar Wilde, was part of the fin-de-siècle disturbance of gender. While dandies and decadents undermined 'muscular' masculinity, the New Woman '*was perceived as a direct threat to classic Victorian definitions of femininity' (Ledger, 1995). She was a cliché of the press that Stoker's reader would have recognised.

At times, ideas relating to the New Woman were contradictory and confused;

> "On the one hand, she might be associated with the apostles of free love, and excessive sexual activity, but on the other hand she could be condemned for frigidity and a concern for mental development at the expense of her 'natural' physical functions" (Ledger, 1995).

Whether seen as a masculine career-seeker or having a monstrous sexuality, men felt their authority and place in the hierarchy was being undermined by the independent woman. The women linked to this label had differing opinions themselves but were united by the principle that their actions should be dictated by personal choice.

While Mina does have a degree of independence and education which would link her to aspects of the New Woman stereotype, she herself is seen to criticise these women in Chapter 8. She remarks on the 'severe tea' which she enjoyed with Lucy in Whitby and joked how they had appetites to put the New Woman to shame, the link being made between insatiable sexual appetite and over-eating. She then openly criticises the thought that in time the New Woman would probably propose to a man and engage in pre-marital sex. Rather than see as a move to liberty and independence she scoffs *"And a nice job she will make of it too!"*

As a school teacher, Mina has economic independence and is shown to have an independent spirit as the narrative progresses. While virtuous, there is ambivalence in her response to Dracula which could suggest an awakening sexuality. However, she can also be seen to be at the service of men. She seems to meekly accept being left at the asylum, which leaves her vulnerable to Dracula, and her ultimate role is to provide resolution to the status quo by conforming as a wife and mother.

Lucy would seem to be less complex as a character. Our access to her consciousness is limited, with her initial letters to Mina conveying the conventional romantic concerns of a young Victorian woman. She is more affluent than Mina and does not have to work to provide for herself. There is no sense that she has any serious intentions to improve her mind or develop a social purpose in life beyond her marriage.

The text could be seen to deviate from realist treatment with patterning, Lucy's men providing a parallel to Harker's three vampire women. In this sense she is cast as a victim.

Some have read Lucy's flirtatious nature and suggestion *"Why can't they let a girl marry three men, or as many as want her, and save all this trouble?"* (Chapter 5) as evidence of her liberal sexual attitudes. It can also be read as her pride and enjoyment in having three suitors asking for her hand in marriage.

Carol Senf (1997) proposes that

> "*her desire for three husbands suggests a degree of latent sexuality which connects her to the New Woman of the period*"

Pedlar counters that in the context of the text Lucy's wish for 'as many as want her' is an indication of her passive submission to the convention role of wife, rather than expression of independence. Lucy sees her only route as marriage. Her desire not to reject the proposals is not sexual greed, but a social wish to avoid emotional conflict.

On the surface Stoker would seem to insist on defending the purity of women. The male characters need to protect them from vampires. However, it is not as simple as this. Mina's admission that she did not wish to hinder Dracula's approach suggests that it is not only external threats which need to be avoided. Vampire folklore requires the vampire to be invited in. The victim becomes complicit and for that shares responsibility. Like Mina, Jonathan Harker enters the castle '*freely and of his own will*'. Both are complicit, although it can be argued not fully aware of the dangers faced.

In Lucy's encounter with Dracula, she only recalls the eyes, with her description relying on sensory perceptions; "*something very sweet and bitter around me... there was a sort of agonising feeling, as if I were in an earthquake*" (Chapter 8).

As with the other characters exposed to the vampire, she is ambivalent. The singing reflects a laugh. Lucy differs in that her experience incorporates natural phenomena, with the deep sea and earthquake suggesting an overwhelming experience. Those who apply dream analysis to her account suggest there is phallic imagery in the lighthouse. However, her recollection has a spiritual element as well, as her soul seems to leave her body.

Lucy's sleepwalking, combined with her description of some form of projection chimed with Victorian though on manifestations of the mind and spirit. When sleepwalking the mind is freed from conscious restraints and the walker is guided by sensory perceptions, with the body acting automatically. Lucy's sleepwalking has existed since her childhood, and for some readers would also be seen as a marker of her vulnerability to suggestion. Sleepwalking, or somnambulism, was linked to hypnotism and lack of control of self.

Lucy sleepwalks into Dracula's arms. It can be argued that as a desiring and desired woman he has responded to her need and that this is evidence that she is a 'wanton' New Woman, more so than Mina with her economic and intellectual independence. Whether seen as innocent girl or knowing, immoral woman, Lucy does suffer a violent end as a result of her loss of control of self.

Hysteria, hypnotism and loss of self

Later in the text it is Mina who is hypnotised by Van Helsing in a bid to track down Dracula. Both Mina and Jonathan have fallen under the hypnotic power of the vampire. Earlier in the century, mesmerism had been used in a medical context but had fallen into disrepute when some practitioners exploited patients and invited audiences to witness them in a hypnotised state. Stoker references Jean-Martin Charcot, who had used hypnotism in the 1870s as a treatment for women suffering from 'hysteria'. The name 'hysteria' derives from the Greek work *hustera*, meaning womb, and it took the shellshock experienced by men in World War I for the medical profession to realise that what we now know as PTSD was not a female-only affliction.

It is interesting to note that Stoker carefully chooses to use the word 'hypnotism', the key difference being hypnotism requires the co-operation of the subject. This may suggest that the victims are complicit in their fate. The links to hypnotism are telling. Charcot has shown that while impairment of physical movement, breathing and speech were genuine, they had roots in psychological rather than physical causes. Most were linked with fearfulness and a lack of will.

Gendered Readings: Conclusion

Readings of gender and sex in the novel note the possibility of reading vampirism as an allegory for the spread of contagious sexual diseases such as syphilis. Sexuality is represented in polar opposition through Lucy and Mina. Lucy who is flirtatious and jokes about marrying all three of her suitors is vulnerable to the vampire. Mina is seen as a beacon of purity and is able to resist, although she exposes herself when Dracula punishes her for venturing into the masculine world of knowledge.

It is the male characters who must restore balance by staking the heart of the vampire.

The Vampyre

4.4 Historicist and Post-colonial Readings

In this section we will;
- *Demonstrate understanding of the significance and influence of the contexts in which literary texts are written and received*
- *Explore connections across literary texts and contexts*
- *To show understanding of how Stoker's choice of form, structure and language shapes meanings.*

Dracula and Historicist Approaches

While drawing on anthropological models and old superstitions, Stoker's story is firmly set in modern London. The text has been read by Daniel Pick in his essay 'Terrors of the Night' as:

"articulating a vision of the bio-medical degeneration of the race in general and the metropolitan population in particular"(Pick,1988).

The text does not explicitly present anxieties about sexuality or social fears. The novel draws on themes of resistance, frustration, and failure of insight. Seward is a practitioner of orthodox medicine. Even when faced with Lucy's unusual and rapid deterioration he is reluctant to diagnose unconventional or supernatural aspects.

The text was published in the decades following a public interest in hysteria and hypnotism. As hypnotism was exploited as an entertainment there was a public concern about the abuse of such techniques, and fears that the unconscious could be induced to crime. It could be argued that in Dracula and Van Helsing we see a battle of hypnotic powers.

The text has a concern to locate the dividing line between sanity and insanity. Often this is aligned with oppositions between purity and corruption. Ultimately the text suggests that there is not a division but a spectrum, and that control of sanity and purity is tenuous.

Victorian readers had already experienced a shock in Darwin's theory that we are not evolutionarily separate from animals. Stoker makes reference to the investigations into atavism and degeneration presented by Max Nordau and Cesare Lambroso.

The perceived social and political dangers are imposed on the foreign Count. This is not fully resolved as a force has arrived which is

"distorting the name and body of the West (Lucy Westenra), transmitting unknown poisons from blood to blood" (Pick, 1988).

The narrative resists and ignores, as seen in Seward's disbelief and Mina choosing not to read Harker's diary. Characters would seem to become hysterical at points where they cannot rationalise what they are witnessing. Pick saw the uncertainty in Stoker's text as a reflection of developments in psychology, as psychiatry moved further in its exploration of the unconscious.

The heroes of the text reject conventional science not to move to the future but to return to folklore. Harker's journal reflects popular theories of degeneracy. He notes his impressions of those he meets with a taxonomy of 'defects', for example observing that the Slovaks had prominent cases of goitre. This was a trait considered to indicate corruption, and here Harker applies the shaky 'science' of physiognomy to an entire nation.

The purpose of Lambroso's work linking physiognomy and degeneracy had been to attempt to identify delinquency through examination of physical attributes. In the 1890s these methods were ridiculed by medical experts. It was no longer believed that 'handle' ears or bushy eyebrows had any correlation with criminality. However, the idea of a criminal 'type' survived and was now believed to be an anomaly of blood, brain or nervous system. Stoker uses the idea of blood pollution as an allegory and a way to present the vampire in a modern setting.

In some ways Dracula harks back to earlier fears as Dracula is full of references to physiognomy. However, the text often debunks this approach as counter-productive, as things are not what they seem.

Harker's first description of Dracula does seem to focus on his unusual physical attributes. In a novel which provides metaphors for contemporary sexual and political discourses there would seem to be support of Halberstrom's critique of the implied anti-Semitism, as when Van Helsing is dismissive of the man who helped Dracula escape the final chase, with reference to his Jewish faith suggesting this was a factor.

What is evident is that Harker drew on the contemporary pejorative image of the parasite. This image was linked to criminology and was seriously discussed as a model by people such as Lanhester, a curator of the British Museum, who published a 'revision' of Darwin which argued that in the city of London, 'devolution' aided survival in a noxious and dangerous city and that groups of people resorted to crime and parasitic behaviour to survive. At government level, there were real fears that the population were becoming weaker and physically stunted. A medical debate was presented as to whether each generation would have weaker offspring or the nation would become sterile. Jonathan Harker's vision of Dracula's arrival in London creating *"a new and ever-widening circle of semi-demons"* links to the fears about the growth of an underclass.

The fear of genetic weakness links to the ideas that although the degenerate may inherit an affliction, they then hold the responsibility of passing it on to the next generation.

Harker could be seen as weak in relation to willpower and desire. He puts himself in danger by ignoring Dracula's warnings and exploring the parts of the castle where the female vampires reside.

Pick saw a link between Harker's imprisonment and Victorian uncertainty:

"The novel in part explored and was in part imprisoned by its own situation...on the verge of the new century, in a kind of corridor between different forms of knowledge and understanding" (Pick, 1988).

On one hand the text could be seen to sensationalise degeneration as they heartily pursue Dracula and his 'child brain'. On the other, it could be seen to confine and contain fears within the text.

It is interesting to consider the text in the light of Stoker's later work. Within ten years of publication, much of the work surrounding degeneration had been soundly rejected, yet fears of foreign influence were still in evidence in the strengthened *Immigration Act of 1905*.

Stoker's 1905 novel *The Man* explicitly engaged in arguments about female beauty, pride and self-reliance as the foundations for 'good stock', with male characters admired for strength, intelligence and bravery. The novel engages with debates on sex versus gender as the female character is christened Stephen Norman by parents who wished for a son, and later puts herself in social jeopardy by proposing to the wrong man. She very much seems to be the 'New Woman' that Mina warns of at her Whitby tea.

Daniel Pick argues that by 1905 *"the veil of the vampire can now be seen through"*. Stoker no longer needs the allegory of Dracula - it is in the insecurities and interactions of humans that we see *"the tortures and terrors of the night"*.

Dracula makes his own community. His connections are literally 'blood ties' - ambiguous with Harker, it is certainly the link with Lucy and Mina. While Dracula is a European, the text stresses that he is from the Eastern limits and is part of a Catholic and superstitious community. He operates as an older, feudal lord. His appetites are unrestrained, attributed to his 'child's brain'. He is seen as degenerate, uncontrolled, lacking in civilisation despite his ancestry. Mina and Van Helsing discussed how they will successfully foil Dracula's plan as he is only capable of plotting one thing at a time, whereas this 'crew of light' can innovate. Dracula lacks community and nationality - he is isolated and the band of brothers will defeat him.

> **TASK: Historicist Approaches**
>
> "...The Count represents precisely those dark secret desires drives that the men most fear in themselves, which are most destructive to both poles of identity - the intimate self of the family man, threatened by unrestrained sexual appetites, and the communal self of the nation, undermined by violent internal competition more than by external invasion"
>
> Daniel Pick, Terrors of the Night
>
> To what extent would you support Pick's interpretation of Count Dracula?
>
> You should consider:
> - Language and imagery used to describe Dracula and his action
> - How other characters respond to Dracula's
> - Expression of fears in the novel

As with Lucy, Dracula's death is a communal event. He is also seen to have a final look of peace. If the vampires are testament to the terrifying powers of degeneracy, then the Harkers "*exemplify the difficulties and rewards of resistance*".

Solitude is seen as a morally vulnerable state. Jonathan Harker is alone in the castle and this places him in danger. He is passive and at one point is 'saved' by Dracula, although he is threatened by his love.

Marriage was seen as sanctifying the maternal, supported by Victorian views. Mina does not fall victim to own desires but is placed in dangerous solitude when the men leave her alone in the asylum. To the Victorian, sexual desire was worse than an actual transgression. Mina's danger comes from her admission that she did not resist Dracula, and this leads to her guilt and revulsion. When she is included in the group she is able to exert her will and defeat his power.

Dracula is an example of Urban Gothic as it concludes with disruptive elements expelled and stable categories of family reaffirmed. The text reflects developments in individual and collective identity. It is the community that conquers the vampire. The text presents a scientific conquest and it is worth noting that the text reads like a detective story rather than a ghost story, and Stoker was influenced by Wilkie Collins and termed his own work 'a mystery'.

Traditionally, Gothic texts relied on shared, communal knowledge of supernatural and accepted superstition and religious belief. In the Urban Gothic "no implicit knowledge; everything must be tested and proved". There is an attempt to use empirical methods to address the supernatural. One effect is that the text often affirms the supernatural as it attempts to expel it. Dracula is a formless attacker yet Stoker "*has given to formlessness itself a form of continuing potency*".

Dracula and Capitalism

Some critics have argued that more than the moral outrage there is anger that Dracula does not circulate his wealth. He may buy houses but he does not invest in England, his vampirism a "monstrous anti-capitalism" which is an affront to a struggling country in the grips of recession. There are echoes in the text of an attack made by Marx on capitalist industry, which he accuses of sucking the blood of children and vulnerable workers in dangerous factories. People are commodities in Victorian capitalism and Dracula is a Gothic embodiment of the abuse of power.

Diametrically opposed to Dracula we are presented with Lucy and Mina who serve to represent Englishness as a form of quiet femininity and maternal domesticity which is most under threat.

It could be argued that by the 1890s the construct of *'Other'* was moving from a purely religious, racial or ethnic intolerance to a wider prejudice towards outsiders fuelled by the pseudo-science of degeneration theories, themselves a mis-reading of Darwin's evolution model as proof of 'devolution'.

The other and doubling: 'The Unseen Face in the Mirror'

In her essay 'The Unseen Face in the Mirror' Carol Senf proposes that Dracula is more than a mythic re-enactment of Good and Evil typical of traditional 'monster' fiction. In the Preface the reader is told information will be *"given from the standpoints and within the range of knowledge of those who made them"*. The narration does not allow writer to comment on failure of judgement and lack of self-knowledge. This gives clues of unreliability.

Harker's conclusion provides an example of a narrator questioning their own reliability through an explicit question. The questioning of sanity links to unreliability. More than half of the novel is set in or around the asylum.

Senf argues that the main characters are young and inexperienced, and only distinguished by professions. It is felt Stoker *"maintains a consistency of style"* and presents the ordinary confronted with extraordinary.

The text gives Dracula humanising touches, although he is never seen objectively and is not allowed to speak for self. Dracula is never given a chance to explain and he is condemned by the English characters' subjective responses to him and the way of life he represents.

Some readers have playfully argued that the killings of the Demeter's crew cannot be proven and that Lucy's death could equally have been as a result of the blood transfusions; given it was a new technology at that time.

A key moment is in the early chapters as Harker looks in the mirror. Dracula is close yet there is *"no reflection of him in the mirror...no sign of a man in it, except myself"*. This lack of reflection has been interpreted as a metaphor for Harker's own lack of moral vision. Harker cannot identify his own weaknesses. He is very much the parochial Englishman. His initial curiosity seems to be only to confirm preconceptions. Harker sees Dracula as a feudal anachronism.

Harker's journal seems to reproduce Dracula's pride and individualism. There is a sudden shift as Harker fears reverse imperialism. He is fearful of his own projected image of Dracula's capacity to create an "*ever-widening circle of semi-demons*".

Harker seems demonic himself when he attacks Dracula while sleeping. He becomes violent and irrational. Likewise, Mina's later criticism of Dracula's criminal brain and blinkered purpose could equally refer to the group's own habits.

Senf posits that:

"*Stoker implies that the only difference between Dracula and his opponents is the narrator's ability to state individual desire in terms of what they believe is a common goal*" (Senf,1997)

It should be remembered that Dracula is an internal rather than an external threat. He must be invited in. Van Helsing warns the group of temptations and desires. Various narrators explain that their hatred is due to a variety of reasons.

Dracula is:

"*relying on the others' desires to emulate his freedom from external constraints*" (Senf,1997)

Like Renfield's wish for immortality, Lucy's escape from upper class existence is a wish to escape religion and law.

Imperial Gothic: Presentation of race in *Dracula*

Further reading:

Judith Halberstrom

Technologies of Monstrosity: Bram Stoker's Dracula

Halberstrom presents a thought-provoking interpretation of the text which notes the potential to trace anti-Semitism in the references to Dracula's physical appearance and accumulation of money and assets. Jonathan, Mina and the zookeeper make reference to Dracula's facial features, recalling the work of Nordau and Lambroso, who had argued certain features or expressions could be a sign of criminality. Halberstrom notes that Stoker had been a friend and acquaintance of Richard Burton, who had written a tract reviving arguments about blood libel and stoked antagonism towards London Jews.

Foucault also makes links between the popularity of vampire novels and the rise in racism encouraged by the myth of threats to 'blood'. However, he sees it in a socialist framework. Earlier vampire novels had focused on the vampire as an aristocrat, preying on the weak and less powerful classes. Now the threat was from those perceived as 'different' or 'other'. Dracula sits at the boundary of this change, being both an aristocrat and a foreign immigrant.

Halberstrom also notes that in many texts the Gothic monster can be seen as an aggregate of race, class and gender:

"*Gothic monsters in particular, produce monstrosity as never unitary, but always as an aggregate of 'race', class and gender*". She further argues that monstrosity her is "*a mixture of bad blood, unstable gender identity, sexual and economic parasitism and degeneracy*".

Halberstrom argues for Gothic texts to be seen in their historical contexts, as each 'monster' is a temporary response to particular social, political or interpersonal problems of a given time.

Anti-Semitism in the text

The brief reference made to "*ole Jerusalem*" by the worker employed to move the boxes of earth provides some evidence of reference to the smell of decay as a racial comment linking smell and pollution. Halberstrom notes this as 'Gothic economy', which serves to condense monstrous traits in a single being-

"*Dracula is otherness itself*"

(Halberstrom,1993).

The 'Other' in Gothic fiction is often drawn from science and popular discourse. Here, Halberstrom feels Stoker draws on late Victorian prejudices against the East London Jews, who were seen as flourishing economically in a time of depression, and were accused of making profit of others' misfortune. While a supernatural text, Dracula is often linked to material goods and images of capitalism. Harker discovers large amounts of gold from various countries in the castle, and in Piccadilly a failed attempt to stab Dracula causes him to 'bleed' gold as money falls from his pockets.

Dracula as invasion text

Throughout the text, social stability is undermined and Dracula serves to attack both women and national pride in his successful seduction through use of a foreign sexuality. Halberstrom argues that:

"*In Dracula, vampires are precisely a 'race' and a family that weakens the stock of Englishness by passing on degeneracy and the disease of blood lust*".

Dracula is a parasite who feeds on English wealth and health. This image is presented by Harker, who envisages Dracula like a leech who will feed on the population of London. For Harker, Dracula represents an aristocratic tyranny and the worst of foreign corruption. A further irony is that Harker himself must use money in the form of bribes and arranging a race by railway to protect Mina and vanquish the threat.

Halberstrom sees echoes of *The Merchant of Venice* in Stoker's portrayal of the count and in his inversion of Shylock's speech, as Dracula proudly asserts his difference to others and his superior race. Dracula is a figure of hate as Shylock is; "*his function within a Gothic economy is to be all difference to all people*".

Embedded in the opposition is the idea of an unhealthy or unnatural sexuality. Where Lucy is punished for expressing desire for three men, Mina is offered as a maternal role who offers a nurturing and acceptable sexuality. She is saved from the pathological vampire by conforming to the normal role of mother.

Various critics have read the relationships between other characters and the vampire as homosexual, heterosexual, exogamic and homoerotic. As well as producing these varied meanings, the vampire reproduces his own kind. The women may feed but they do not reproduce. They do present a blend of power and femininity which threatens the male characters, as does Dracula's ability to mesmerise the women.

Throughout the text, it is Dracula who is virile, of good blood and able to reproduce. It is only in conquering him and in having a child that Harker can reclaim his security. Ironically, the encounters with the vampire and the transfusions required to aid Lucy have allowed the possibility that all of the male characters have fathered Quincey Harker through the mixing of blood. It remains the final ambiguity that in asserting the success of good and moral blood Harker reminds the reader that Dracula's blood also flows through Mina and the next generation. In addition, the child is named after an American - Englishness can no longer claim a singular lineage or power.

Throughout the text, there is a focus on modes of production and consumption. While Dracula is a composite otherness, the text itself is a composite or multi-strand narrative constructed of various forms of writing and recording. Mina takes charge of ordering the narrative, channelling energy into reading and writing. Reading is offered as a safe space for disclosure and characters take each other into confidence through reading each other's thoughts. This is most evident when Mina completes her transcript of Seward's recordings and she notes his emotions, while promising to protect him from exposure in her notes. Reading and writing provide a safe form of interaction in stark contrast to the vampire's sharing and mingling of blood.

Genre and History: New Historicism

Academic and critic Valerie Pedlar (2001) presents a new historicist approach in her essay *'Dracula: Narrative Strategies and Nineteenth Century Fears'*. Many twentieth century readings focus on the representation of sex and sexuality in the text, and perhaps in doing so overlook analysis of narrative and genre. The text has been referred to as a fiction, a horror, or as a Gothic fantasy. Stoker himself subtitled the text as a 'mystery' story. The text had influenced the vampire genre and for Pedlar has *"attained the status of a myth"*.

Towards the end of the twentieth century, attention turned to the historical, social and cultural contexts in which the text was produced and received. A number of critics agreed that the novel iterated *"concerns about manly women and feminized men, and to fears of degeneracy and invasion"* (Pedlar, 2001).

Phyllis A Roth, in her 1977 reading 'Suddenly Sexual Women', does not attribute this fear of difference to the older Van Helsing, although when comparing to Harker argues

"Van Helsing falls prey to the same attempted seduction by, and the same ambivalence towards, the three vampires" (Roth, 2001).

Pedlar counters that the women are not interested in seducing Van Helsing and it is Mina who is the object of their attention at the campfire. She sees the root of Van Helsing's fears as fear for Mina and the temptation for her to join the others. He has some fear that he may be drawn to their charms.

Pedlar argues Van Helsing's reactions recall Harker's early temptations. He experiences some desire for the female vampires but age and experience enable him to control his feelings and act.

He is a father figure to all and would seem to reinforce patriarchal structures: *"Van Helsing can be seen as a father-figure, and his aim is to restore patriarchal control, with women kept firmly in their place"*.

Post-colonialism in the text

It is only in the last 40 years that critical approaches moved beyond broadly psychoanalytical readings. While there had been some focus on historical contexts, readings often took suppression of desire as the key focus. It can be argued that the text's specific references to its time of publication have aided its enduring appeal.

Initially, this was the aspect that proved disconcerting to original readers. *The Spectator* in 1897 was ambivalent about the "up-to-dateness" of the text.

Dracula appeared soon after Victoria's Jubilee year. Unlike the earlier Jubilee, there were a number of anxieties. England saw a declining global influence. It suffered loss of overseas markets. Germany and the United States were rising politically, and there was continued unrest in remaining colonies. The country was locked in a sense of irretrievable decline. The narrative can be seen as a response to cultural guilt.

The vampire sets out to displace. The men respond by seeking to exterminate. This is seen as heroic act in novel. Throughout oppositions are made between civilisation and atavism. It serves to delimit boundaries.

Dracula represents the savage and atavistic elements of society. He is dangerous yet attractive. Throughout Stoker's fiction there are invasions and historical colonisations referenced, with a specific focus on threats to British Isles. Other texts present a fear of women as anarchic and powerful. Imperial decline can be traced as a theme.

Dracula succeeds in merging Gothic fantasy with contemporary politics. Transylvania formed part of the troubled "Eastern Question" which dogged foreign policy of the 1880s and 1890s. Armenians had massacred Turkish groups in 1894 and 1896. The Carpathians were a centre for political conflict in which the cycle of Empire was enacted - the rise, decay, collapse and displacement. England was also feared to be decaying and on the point of collapse.

Dracula's own racial and ethnic background is ambiguous. He is proud of his Szekely past and was at the forefront of racial conquest and domination. While he now functions as a vampire, he is not the weakened vampire of tradition but a vigorous and threatening presence. There was a natural link between collapse of empire and vampirism. When Dracula moves to London he relocates the struggle to Britain, and threatens to penetrate London, the heart of empire, with his "semi-demons". Dracula's lust for blood is a combination of the vampire's need for sustenance and the warrior's desire for conquest. He endangers the nation and jeopardises personal integrity.

Dracula presents a dual threat, political and biological. His aggression is against both the body and the body politic. Vampirism is a colonisation of the body. The horror is not in the destruction of but the transformation of bodies. Allowing blood to equate with race, Dracula sucks blood and literally deracinates. He will destroy the human race.

Dracula is more robust that the English men who challenge him. The alarming decline of the British seems to invigorate the female victims. Lucy becomes bright and cheery while Harker becomes pale and exhausted. Harker and Dracula transpose as the novel progresses.

The fact that Van Helsing makes them 'sterilise' the boxes of earth aligns Dracula's threat with a dangerous fertility. The text has fathers that are dead or dying. The younger men are not fathers in the text. Mina and Jonathan do have a child at the close of the text, but have been marked and changed by the infection of vampirism. While they have started a family there is an ambiguity - one reading is that the child reminds the men of their shared experience and eventual success. An alternative reading is that the weakened British race has to generate vicariously, and the child is named after the American Quincey.

Appendices

Examples of Examination Tasks

This appendix provides some examples of questions on Dracula set by various examination boards. Further examples can be found on each examination board's website.

AQA LANGUAGE AND LITERATURE A LEVEL 7707 PAPER 1

Read the extract printed below. This is from the section of the novel where Jonathan Harker writes about his coach journey to Dracula's castle.

Explore the significance of Harker's journal in the novel.
You should consider:
• the presentation of Harker's point of view in the extract below and at different points of the novel.
• the use of fantasy elements in constructing a fictional world.

> *Soon we were hemmed in with trees, which in places arched right over the roadway till we passed as through a tunnel; and again great frowning rocks guarded us boldly on either side. Though we were in shelter, we could hear the rising wind, for it moaned and whistled through the rocks, and the branches of the trees crashed together as we swept along. It grew colder and colder still, and fine, powdery snow began to fall, so that soon we and all around us were covered with a white blanket. The keen wind still carried the howling of the dogs, though this grew fainter as we went on our way. The baying of the wolves sounded nearer and nearer, as though they were closing round on us from every side. I grew dreadfully afraid, and the horses shared my fear; but the driver was not in the least disturbed. He kept turning his head to left and right, but I could not see anything through the darkness. Suddenly, away on our left, I saw a faint flickering blue flame. The driver saw it at the same moment; he at once checked the horses and, jumping to the ground, disappeared into the darkness. I did not know what to do, the less as the howling of the wolves grew closer; but while I wondered the driver suddenly appeared again, and without a word took his seat, and we resumed our journey. I think I must have fallen asleep and kept dreaming of the incident, for it seemed to be repeated endlessly, and now looking back, it is like a sort of awful nightmare.*

AQA A LEVEL LANGUAGE AND LITERATURE 7707/1 Telling Stories

Read the extract printed below. This is from the section of the novel where Mina describes how she is worried about Lucy's deteriorating health

Explore the significance of Lucy's physical state in the novel.

You should consider:
• the presentation of Lucy's physical state in the extract below and at different points of the novel
• the use of fantasy elements in constructing a fictional world.

> When coming home – it was then bright moonlight, so bright that, though the front of our part of the Crescent was in shadow, everything could be well seen – I threw a glance up at our window, and saw Lucy's head leaning out. I thought that perhaps she was looking out for me, so I opened my handkerchief and waved it. She did not notice or make any movement whatever. Just then, the moonlight crept round an angle of the building, and the light fell on the window. There distinctly was Lucy with her head lying up against the side of the windowsill and her eyes shut. She was fast asleep, and by her, seated on the window-sill, was something that looked like a good-sized bird. I was afraid she might get a chill, so I ran upstairs, but as I came into the room she was moving back to her bed, fast asleep, and breathing heavily; she was holding her hand to her throat, as though to protect it from cold. I did not wake her, but tucked her up warmly; I have taken care that the door is locked and the window securely fastened. She looks so sweet as she sleeps; but she is paler than is her wont, and there is a drawn, haggard look under her eyes which I do not like. I fear she is fretting about something. I wish I could find out what it is.

AQA A LEVEL LANGUAGE AND LITERATURE 7707/1 Telling Stories

Read the extract printed below. This is from the section of the novel where Jonathan Harker describes the men's visit to Carfax.
Explore the significance of Carfax as a location in the novel.

You should consider:
- the presentation of Carfax in the extract below and at different points in the novel
- the use of fantasy elements in constructing a fictional world.

> The whole place was thick with dust. The floor was seemingly inches deep, except where there were recent footsteps, in which on holding down my lamp I could see marks of hobnails where the dust was caked. The walls were fluffy and heavy with dust, and in the corners were masses of spiders' webs, whereon the dust had gathered till they looked like old tattered rags as the weight had torn them partly down. On a table in the hall was a great bunch of keys, with a time-yellowed label on each. They had been used several times, for on the table were several similar rents in the blanket of dust, similar to that exposed when the Professor lifted them. He turned to me and said:– 'You know this place, Jonathan. You have copied maps of it, and you know at least more than we do. Which is the way to the chapel?' I had an idea of its direction, though on my former visit I had not been able to get admission to it; so I led the way, and after a few wrong turnings found myself opposite a low, arched oaken door, ribbed with iron bands. 'This is the spot,' said the Professor as he turned his lamp on a small map of the house, copied from the file of my original correspondence regarding the purchase. With a little trouble we found the key on the bunch and opened the door. We were prepared for some unpleasantness, for as we were opening the door a faint, malodorous air seemed to exhale through the gaps, but none of us ever expected such an odour as we encountered.

AQA A LEVEL LANGUAGE AND LITERATURE 7706/1 (AS)

Read the extract printed below.

Examine how Stoker presents Dracula in this extract.

> Within, stood a tall old man, clean-shaven save for a long white moustache, and clad in black from head to foot, without a single speck of colour about him anywhere. He held in his hand an antique silver lamp, in which the flame burned without chimney or globe of any kind, throwing long, quivering shadows as it flickered in the draught of the open door. The old man motioned me in with his right hand with a courtly gesture, saying in excellent English, but with a strange intonation:- 'Welcome to my house! Enter freely and of your own will!' He made no motion of stepping to meet me, but stood like a statue, as though his gesture of welcome had fixed him into stone. The instant, however, that I had stepped over the threshold, he moved impulsively forward, and holding out his hand grasped mine with a strength which made me wince, an effect which was not lessened by the fact that it seemed as cold as ice – more like the hand of a dead than a living man. Again he said:- 'Welcome to my house. Come freely. Go safely. And leave something of the happiness you bring!' The strength of the handshake was so much akin to that which I had noticed in the driver, whose face I had not seen, that for a moment I doubted if it were not the same person to whom I was speaking; so, to make sure, I said interrogatively:- 'Count Dracula?' He bowed in a courtly way as he replied: 'I am Dracula. And I bid you welcome, Mr Harker, to my house. Come in; the night air is chill, and you must need to eat and rest.' As he was speaking he put the lamp on a bracket on the wall, and stepping out, took my luggage; he had carried it in before I could forestall him. I protested, but he insisted:- 'Nay, sir, you are my guest. It is late, and my people are not available. Let me see to your comfort myself.' He insisted on carrying my traps along the passage, and then up a great winding stair, and along another great passage, on whose stone floor our steps rang heavily. At the end of this he threw open a heavy door, and I rejoiced to see within a well-lit room in which a table was spread for supper, and on whose mighty hearth a great fire of logs flamed and flared. The Count halted, putting down my bags, closed the door, and crossing the room, opened another door, which led into a small octagonal room lit by a single lamp, and seemingly without a window of any sort. Passing through this, he opened another door, and motioned me to enter. It was a welcome sight; for here was a great bedroom well lighted and warmed with another log fire, which sent a hollow roar up the wide chimney. The Count himself left my luggage inside and withdrew, saying, before he closed the door:- 'You will need, after your journey, to refresh yourself by making your toilet. I trust you will find all you wish. When you are ready come into the other room, where you will find your supper prepared.'

AQA A LEVEL LANGUAGE AND LITERATURE 7706/1

Read the extract printed below.

Examine how Stoker presents the storm in Whitby in this extract.

> CUTTING FROM THE DAILYGRAPH, 8 AUGUST (Pasted in Mina Murray's Journal)
>
> From a Correspondent Whitby. [paragraphs omitted]
> Then without warning the tempest broke. With a rapidity which, at the time, seemed incredible, and even afterwards is impossible to realize, the whole aspect of nature at once became convulsed. The waves rose in growing fury, each overtopping its fellow, till in a very few minutes the lately glassy sea was like a roaring and devouring monster. White-crested waves beat madly on the level sands and rushed up the shelving cliffs; others broke over the piers, and with their spume swept the lanthorns of the lighthouses which rise from the end of either pier of Whitby Harbour. The wind roared like thunder, and blew with such force that it was with difficulty that even strong men kept their feet, or clung with grim clasp to the iron stanchions. It was found necessary to clear the entire piers from the mass of onlookers, or else the fatalities of the night would have been increased manifold. To add to the difficulties and dangers of the time, masses of sea-fog came drifting inland – white, wet clouds, which swept by in ghostly fashion, so dank and cold that it needed but little effort of imagination to think that the spirits of those lost at sea were touching their living brethren with the clammy hands of death, and many a one shuddered as the wreaths of sea-mist swept by. At times the mist cleared, and the sea for some distance could be seen in the glare of the lightning, which now came thick and fast, followed by such sudden peals of thunder that the whole sky overhead seemed trembling under the shock of the footsteps of the storm. Some of the scenes thus revealed were of immeasurable grandeur and of absorbing interest – the sea, running mountains high, threw skywards with each wave mighty masses of white foam, which the tempest seemed to snatch at and whirl away into space; here and there a fishing-boat, with a rag of sail, running madly for shelter before the blast; now and again the white wings of a storm-tossed sea-bird. On the summit of the East Cliff the new searchlight was ready for experiment, but had not yet been tried. The officers in charge of it got it into working order, and in the pauses of the inrushing mist swept with it the surface of the sea. Once or twice its service was most effective, as when a fishing-boat, with gunwale under water, rushed into the harbour, able, by the guidance of the sheltering light, to avoid the danger of dashing against the piers. As each boat achieved the safety of the port there was a shout of joy from the mass of people on shore, a shout which for a moment seemed to cleave the gale and was then swept away in its rush.

OCR A Level H472/02: Comparative and contextual study (Component 02)

This question requires you to compare characteristics of two related texts.

You can adapt responses to focus solely on *Dracula*.

a) 'Gothic writing frequently explores the battle between good and evil.'

Consider how far you agree with this statement by comparing *Dracula* with at least one other text prescribed for this topic.

b) 'Suspense is a key feature of narrative in Gothic writing.'

By comparing at least two texts prescribed for this topic, discuss how far you have found this to be the case. In your answer you must include discussion of *Dracula*.

c) 'The conflict between reason and emotion is characteristically Gothic.'

Consider how far you agree with this statement by comparing *Dracula* with at least one other text prescribed for this topic.

d) 'Innocence is often an important element in Gothic writing.'

Compare its uses and effects in *Dracula* with those in at least one other text prescribed for this topic.

e) 'Setting is always a key aspect of Gothic writing.'

By comparing at least two texts prescribed for this topic, discuss how far you have found this to be the case. In your answer you must include discussion of *Dracula*.

EDEXCEL A LEVEL 9ET02

In your answer you must consider the following:

- the writers' methods
- links between the texts
- the relevance of contextual factors.

  a) Compare the ways in which the writers of your two chosen texts create **a sense of fear** in their works. You must relate your discussion to relevant contextual factors.

  b) Compare the ways in which **settings are created and used** by the writers of your two chosen texts. You must relate your discussion to relevant contextual factors.

  c) Compare the ways in which the writers of your two chosen texts convey **the threat or presence of death**.

  d) Compare the ways in which the writers of your two chosen texts **make use of significant locations** in their texts.

  e) Compare the ways in which the writers of your two chosen texts present **characters who experience anxiety**.

  f) Compare the ways in which the writers of your two chosen texts **examine violence**. You must relate your discussion to relevant contextual factors.

EDEXCEL AS LEVEL 8ET02 PROSE (AS)

  a) Compare the ways in which the writers of your two chosen texts present **cruelty.**

  b) Compare the ways in which the writers of your two chosen texts present **masculinity**.

CCEA NI Unit AS 2: The Study of Prose Pre 1900

Students should be able to:

- articulate informed and relevant responses that communicate effectively their knowledge and understanding of a novel
- analyse the writer's use of narrative methods such as structure, form and language
- demonstrate understanding of the significance and influence of the contexts in which a novel is written and received, by drawing on appropriate information from outside the novel
- explore a novel informed by different interpretations

a) Mina Harker is a woman in need of constant protection.

With reference to Stoker's narrative methods, and relevant contextual information, show to what extent you agree with the above statement.

b) Dracula is a novel about the victory of good over evil.

With reference to Stoker's narrative methods, and relevant contextual information, show to what extent you agree with the above statement.

c) Dracula does little more than play upon the fears of late-nineteenth-century society.

With reference to Stoker's narrative methods, and relevant contextual information, show to what extent you agree with the above statement.

d) In Dracula, Stoker challenges the nineteenth-century view of men as powerful.

With reference to Stoker's narrative methods, and relevant contextual information, show to what extent you agree with the above statement.

References for Wider Reading

Arata, S. (1990) 'The Occidental Tourist: 'Dracula' and the Anxiety of Reverse Colonization', *Victorian Studies* Vol 33 Issue 4, pp. 621-645.

Belford, B. (1996) *Bram Stoker: a biography of the author of Dracula*. London : Weidenfeld and Nicolson, 1996.

Bloom, H. (2003) *Modern Critical Interpretations: Bram Stoker's Dracula*, London: Chelsea House, 2003.

Halberstrom, J. (1993) 'Technologies of Monstrosity: Bram Stoker's Dracula', *Victorian Studies*, Vol. 36, No. 3, *Victorian Sexualities* (Spring, 1993), pp. 333-352.

Jackson, R. (1981) *Fantasy: The Literature of Subversion*. London: Routledge, 2015.

Ledger, S. (2011) *Cultural Politics at the Fin de Siècle*. Cambridge: Cambridge University Press, 2011.

Pedlar, V. (2001) '*Dracula*: a fin-de-siècle fantasy' in *The Nineteenth Century Novel: Identities*, London : Routledge, 2001.

Pedlar, V. (2001) 'Dracula: narrative strategies and nineteenth-century fears' in *The Nineteenth Century Novel: Identities*, London : Routledge, 2001.

Pick, D. (1988) 'Terrors of the Night', *Critical Quarterly*, Vol 3 Issue 4, pp. 71-87, 1988

Punter, D. (1980, 1996) *The Literature of Terror,* London: Longman, 1996.

Roth, P. (1997) 'Suddenly Sexual Women in Bram Stoker's *Dracula*' in *Bloom's Modern Critical Interpretations: Bram Stoker's Dracula*, Chelsea House, 2003.

Schleifer, R. (1980) 'The Trap of the Imagination', Criticism, Volume 22 Issue 4, pp. 297-319.

Senf, C. (1979) 'Dracula: The Unseen Face in the Mirror', *The Journal of Narrative Technique*, Vol. 9, No. 3 (Autumn, 1979), pp. 160-170.

Spencer, K. (1992) *Purity and Danger: Dracula, the Urban Gothic and the Late Victorian Degeneracy Crisis, ELH,* Vol. 59, No. 1 (Spring, 1992), pp. 197-225

Terms and Conditions

Copyright Information

Every effort is made to ensure that the information provided in this publication is accurate and up to date but no legal responsibility is accepted for any errors, omissions or misleading statements. It is Athena Online Education's policy to obtain permission for any copyright material in their publications. The publishers will be glad to make suitable arrangements with any copyright holders whom it has not been possible to contact.

Students and teachers may not use any material or content contained within the published text and incorporate it into a body of work without referencing and acknowledging the source of the material.

Disclaimers

This publication is designed to supplement teaching and learning only. Sample questions may be designed to follow the content of a specification and may also attempt to prepare students for the type of questions they will meet in the examination, but will not attempt to predict future examination questions. Athena Online Education do not make any guarantee as to the results that may be obtained from the use of this publication, or as to the accuracy, reliability or content of the publication.

Where a teacher or tutor uses any of the material from this resource to support examinations or similar then the teacher or tutor must ensure that they are happy with the level of information and support provided pertaining to their personal point of view and to the constraints of the specification and to others involved in the delivery of the course. It is considered essential that the teacher or tutor adapt, extend and/or edit any parts of the contained material to suit their needs, the needs of the specification and the needs of the individual or learning group concerned. As such, the teacher or tutor must determine which parts of the material, if any, to provide to the students and which parts to use as background information for themselves. Likewise, the teacher or tutor must determine what additional material is required to cover all points on the specification and to cover each specification point.

Links to other websites, and contextual links are provided where appropriate in Athena Online Education publications. Athena Online Education is not responsible for information on sites that it does not manage, nor can we guarantee, represent or warrant that the content contained in the sites is accurate, legal and inoffensive, nor should a website address or the inclusion of a link be taken to mean endorsement by Athena Online Education of the site to which it points.

Individuals have different personal views on what information and support to provide an individual or group for a given specification and when to provide this. Different specifications and modules require different levels of support or differing amounts of information to be provided, or they prohibit information or support to be given to a student.

Where an individual uses any of the material from this resource to support coursework or similar then the individual must ensure that they are happy with the level of information and support provided pertaining to their personal point of view and to the constraints of the specification and to others involved in moderation or the process or delivery of the course. It is considered essential that the individual adapt, extend and or censor any parts of the contained material to suit their needs, the needs of the specification, the needs of moderators and the needs of the individual or group concerned. As such, the individual must determine which parts of the material, if any, to provide to students and which parts to use as background information for themselves.

Terms and Conditions

The **Terms and Conditions** of this guide include the following acknowledgement:

"You acknowledge that you rely on your own skill and judgement in determining the suitability of the Goods for any particular purpose."

"The publishers do not warrant: that any of the Goods are suitable for any particular purpose (e.g. any particular qualification), or the results that may be obtained from the use of any publication, or expected exam grades, or that the publishers are affiliated with any educational institution, or that any publication is sponsored by, authorised by, associated with, or endorsed by any educational institution."

In summary, it is intended that these materials be used appropriately and at the individual's own discretion. Athena Online Education is not affiliated with DfES, Edexcel, OCR/ UCLES, AQA, WJEC or CCEA in any way nor is this publication authorised by, associated with, sponsored by or endorsed by these institutions unless explicitly stated on the front cover of this publication.

Printed in Great Britain
by Amazon